COOKING
MEASURE FOR MEASURE

All the flavor of regular salt, but only half the sodium.

Creative cookery, with a detailed breakdown of nutrient information for each recipe.

Sixteen days of complete menus.

It's all part of this new MORTON LITE SALT® COOKBOOK: COOKING MEASURE FOR MEASURE. Over 250 recipes show you how to use Morton Lite Salt mixture as regular table salt in cooking, baking and at-the-table seasoning.

Everything from appetizers to meats to casseroles to desserts is highlighted in this 224 page book. Following each recipe, nutrient information is provided on calories, protein, carbohydrates, fats, sodium, potassium and cholesterol. Plus, there's a comprehensive chart listing sodium, potassium and calorie content of popular foods.

The Morton Lite Salt Cookbook

COOKING MEASURE FOR MEASURE

by Frani Shaver Lauda

FAWCETT POPULAR LIBRARY • NEW YORK

COOKING MEASURE FOR MEASURE

Published by Fawcett Popular Library, a unit of CBS Publications, the Consumer Publishing Division of CBS Inc.

ISBN: 0-445-08337-9

Printed in the United States of America

11   10   9   8   7   6   5   4   3   2

CONTENTS

What hymns are sung, what praises said
for homemade miracles of bread. . . .

and other simple but savory fare.

Salt and flavor are almost synonymous with Morton Salt Company, whose little umbrella girl has meant good taste in cooking and at the table for more than a century.

Today, the Morton Salt girl has another fine product for you—Morton Lite Salt, a salt and potassium chloride mixture, the first iodized salt with all the flavor but only half the sodium of regular table salt. Morton Lite Salt is used measure-for-measure in place of regular salt for cooking, baking and at-the-table seasoning.

In recommending this book to you, we remind you that Morton Lite Salt contains sodium and is not a salt substitute. It is not for persons on a sodium or potassium-restricted diet. It's a new way to salt for normal, healthy people.

For your enjoyment, we've developed a collection of recipes kitchen-tested for flavor with Morton Lite Salt. From appetizers through desserts, from everyday through a touch of gourmet, we hope you and your family will like this taste-tempting selection. We've also included daily menu suggestions for each season.

Unique to this cookbook . . . each recipe has been evaluated by a computerized nutrient data bank to determine its per-serving values for the following nutrients: calories, carbohydrates, protein, fats, sodium, potassium and cholesterol. These values are listed immediately after each recipe for your information and convenience.

Bon appetit!

Frani Shaver Lauda

Frani Shaver Lauda

CHAPTER 1

SODIUM/POTASSIUM/ CALORIE COUNTER

CHAPTER 1

SODIUM/POTASSIUM/CALORIE COUNTER

The following chart has been prepared to show the amounts of sodium, potassium and calories contained in the various foods we consume. The figures listed are based on the average portions of these foods commonly eaten.

Meat and Poultry*	Portion	Sodium (mg.)	Potassium (mg.)	Calories
Bacon	1 strip (1 oz.)	71	16	156
Beef				
Corned beef (canned)	3 slices	803	51	184
Hamburger	¼ lb.	41	382	224
Pot roast (rump)	½ lb.	43	309	188
Sirloin steak	½ lb.	57	545	260
Chicken (broiler)	3½ oz.	78	320	151
Duck	3½ oz.	82	285	326
Frankfurter (beef)	⅛ lb.	550	110	129
Ham				
Fresh	¼ lb.	37	260	126
Cured, butt	¼ lb.	518	239	123
Cured, shank	¼ lb.	336	155	91
Lamb				
Shoulder chop	½ lb.	72	422	260
Rib chops (2)	½ lb.	68	398	238
Leg roast	¼ lb.	41	246	96

* Before cooking.

	Portion	Sodium (mg.)	Potassium (mg.)	Calories
Meat and Poultry*				
Liver				
Beef	3½ oz.	86	325	136
Calf	3½ oz.	131	436	141
Pork				
Loin chop	6 oz.	52	500	314
Spareribs (3 or 4)	3½ oz.	51	360	209
Sausage (link or bulk)	3½ oz.	740	140	450
Bologna	3½ oz.	1300	230	304
Turkey	3½ oz.	40	320	268
Veal				
Cutlet	6 oz.	46	448	235
Loin chop	½ lb.	54	384	514
Rump roast	¼ lb.	36	244	84
Fish				
Clams (4 large, 9 small)	3½ oz.	36	235	82
Cod	3½ oz.	70	382	78
Crabmeat	3½ oz.	500	265	100
Flounder or Sole	3½ oz.	56	366	68
Lobster (boiled with 2 tbsp. butter)	¾ lb.	210	180	308
Oysters (5 to 8)				
Fresh	3½ oz.	73	121	66
Frozen	3½ oz.	380	210	66
Salmon (pink, canned)	3½ oz.	387	361	141
Sardines (8, canned in oil)	3½ oz.	510	560	311
Shrimp	3½ oz.	140	220	91
Tuna (canned in oil)	3½ oz.	800	301	288
(canned in water)	3½ oz.	41	279	127
Dairy Products, Margarine				
Butter, salted	1 pat	99	2	72
Butter, unsalted	1 pat	1	2	72
Cheese				
American, Cheddar	1 oz.	197	23	112
American, processed	1 oz.	318	22	107
Cottage, creamed	3½ oz.	229	85	106
Cream, heavy	1 tbsp.	35	10	52
Egg	1 large	66	70	88

*Before cooking.

	Portion	Sodium (mg.)	Potassium (mg.)	Calories
Dairy Products				
Ice cream				
Chocolate	½ pint	75	**	300
Vanilla	½ pint	82	210	290
Milk				
Whole	8 oz.	122	352	159
Skim	8 oz.	130	370	75
Buttermilk	8 oz.	530	410	90
Margarine				
Salted	1 pat	99	2	72
Unsalted	1 tbsp.	0	0	100
Breads, Cereals, etc.				
Bread				
Rye	1 slice	128	33	56
Enriched white	1 slice	117	20	62
Whole wheat	1 slice	121	63	56
Cereals (ready-to-eat)				
Corn flakes	1 cup	165	40	95
Bran flakes	1 cup	920	730	350
Puffed rice, wheat	1 cup	22	229	60
Macaroni, enriched, cooked tender	1 cup	1	85	151
Noodles, enriched, cooked	1 cup	3	70	200
Oatmeal, cooked	1 cup	1	130	148
Pancake, 4-in. diam.	1	425	100	230
Rice, white, dry	¼ cup	3	45	178
Spaghetti, enriched, cooked tender	1 cup	2	92	166
Waffles, enriched	1 waffle	356	109	209
Wheat germ	3 tbsp.	1	232	102
Fruits*				
Apple	1 medium	1	165	87
Apricots				
Fresh	2-3	1	281	51
Canned in syrup	3 halves	1	234	86
Dried	17 halves	26	979	260
Avocado	½	343	340	170
Banana	1, 6-in.	1	370	85
Blueberries	1 cup	1	81	62
Cantaloupe	¼ melon	12	251	30
Cherries				
Fresh	½ cup	2	191	58
Canned in syrup	½ cup	1	124	89

* All portions weigh 3½ oz. unless otherwise noted.
**Data not available.

	Portion	Sodium (mg.)	Potassium (mg.)	Calories
Fruits*				
Dates				
Fresh	10 medium	1	648	274
Dried pitted	1 cup (6 oz.)	2	1150	488
Fruit cocktail	½ cup	5	161	76
Grapefruit	½ medium	1	135	41
Grapes	22	3	158	69
Orange	1 small	1	200	49
Peaches				
Fresh	1 medium	1	202	38
Canned	2 halves, 2 tbsp. syrup	2	130	78
Pears				
Fresh	½ pear	2	130	61
Canned	2 halves, 2 tbsp. syrup	1	84	76
Pineapple				
Fresh	¾ cup	1	146	52
Canned	1 slice and syrup	1	96	74
Plums				
Fresh	2 medium	2	299	66
Canned	3 medium, 2 tbsp. syrup	1	142	83
Prunes				
Dried	10 large	8	694	255
Strawberries	10 large	1	164	37
Watermelon	½ cup	1	100	26
Vegetables				
Artichoke				
Base and soft end of leaves	1 large bud	30	301	44
Asparagus				
Fresh	⅔ cup	1	183	20
Canned	6 spears	271	191	21
Beans, baked	⅝ cup	2	704	159
Beans, canned with pork	½ cup	200	704	159
Beans, green				
Fresh	1 cup	5	189	31
Canned	1 cup	295	109	30
Beans, lima				
Fresh	⅝ cup	1	422	111
Canned	½ cup	271	255	110
Frozen	⅝ cup	129	394	118

*All portions weigh 3½ oz. unless otherwise noted.

	Portion	Sodium (mg.)	Potassium (mg.)	Calories
Vegetables				
Beets				
Fresh	½ cup	36	172	27
Canned	½ cup	196	138	31
Broccoli, fresh	⅔ cup	10	267	26
Brussels sprouts	6-7 medium	10	273	36
Cabbage				
Raw, shredded	1 cup	20	233	24
Cooked	⅗ cup	14	163	20
Carrots				
Raw	1 large	47	341	42
Cooked	⅔ cup	33	222	31
Canned	⅔ cup	236	120	30
Cauliflower	⅞ cup	9	206	22
Celery	1 outer or 3 inner stalks	63	170	8
Corn				
Fresh	1 medium ear	trace	196	100
Canned	½ cup	196	81	70
Cucumber, pared	½ medium	3	80	7
Lettuce, iceberg	3½ oz.	9	264	14
Mushrooms, uncooked	10 small, 4 large	15	414	28
Onions, uncooked	1 medium	10	157	38
Peas				
Fresh	⅔ cup	1	196	71
Canned	¾ cup	236	96	88
Frozen	3½ oz.	115	135	68
Potatoes				
Boiled (in skin)	1 medium	3	407	76
French fried	10 pieces	3	427	137
Radishes	10 small	18	322	17
Sauerkraut	⅔ cup	747	140	18
Spinach	½ cup	45	291	21
Tomatoes				
Raw	1 medium	4	366	33
Canned	½ cup	130	217	21
Paste	3½ oz.	38	888	82

Note: Because vegetable counts vary greatly from raw to cooked state, values are for cooked vegetables with no added salt unless otherwise noted. Frozen vegetables have virtually the same count as fresh vegetables, when cooked, unless otherwise noted.

	Portion	Sodium (mg.)	Potassium (mg.)	Calories
Beverages				
Apple juice	6 oz.	2	187	87
Beer	8 oz.	8	46	114
Coca-Cola	6 oz.	2	88	78
Coffee (brewed)	1 cup	3	149	5
Decaffeinated	1 cup	1–6	80	0
Cranberry cocktail	7 oz.	2	20	130
Ginger ale	8 oz.	18	1	80
Grape juice	3½ oz.	1	120	66
Lemon juice	3½ oz.	1	130	25
Orange juice				
Canned	8 oz.	3	500	120
Fresh	8 oz.	3	496	111
Prune juice	6 oz.	4	423	138
Tea	8 oz.	2	21	2
Whiskey, etc.	1 oz.	1	trace	90
Wine, table	3½ oz.	4–7	20–120	60–120
Snacks, Miscellaneous				
Candy				
Chocolate creams	1 candy	1	15	51
Milk chocolate	1 oz.	30	105	152
Mayonnaise	1 tbsp.	117	9	119
Nuts				
Cashews, roasted	6-8	2	84	84
Peanuts, roasted				
Salted	1 tbsp.	69	105	85
Unsalted	1 tbsp.	trace	111	86
Peanut butter	1 tbsp.	100	110	95
Oil, vegetable	1 tbsp.	0	0	144
Olives				
Green	2 medium	312	7	15
Ripe	2 large	150	5	37
Potato chips	5 chips	34	88	54
Pretzels, 3 ring	1 average	87	7	12
Salt, Morton Lite	¼ tsp.	275	366	0
Salt, regular	¼ tsp.	622	0	0
Salt, substitute	¼ tsp.	0	698	0
Saltines	1 oz.	450	30	100

SOURCES

Church, C. F. and Church, H. N., *Food Values of Portions Commonly Used*, 11th ed. Philadelphia: J. B. Lippincott Co., 1970.

Gormican, A., *Inorganic Elements in Foods Used in Hospital Menus*, J. Am. Diet. Assoc. 56:397-403, May, 1970.

CHAPTER 2

MENUS

CHAPTER 2

MENUS

In the following suggested menus, we have starred the recipes given in this book. To find them, consult the index.

SPRING

DAY 1

BREAKFAST
Grapefruit juice
Shredded wheat
Toast, selected margarine[1]
    and currant jelly
Skim or low-fat milk
Coffee or tea

LUNCH
Lemon-Broiled Chicken*
Rice with Sage*
Italian Carrot and Zucchini
    Salad*
Home-Style Pear Pie*
Skim or low-fat milk
Coffee or tea

DINNER
Beef Carbonnade*
Poppyseed Noodles*
Green Beans*
Pink Grapefruit Salad*
All Whole-Wheat Bread*
    with selected margarine
Silver Cake with White
    Mountain Frosting*
Coffee or tea

DAY 2

BREAKFAST
Orange sections
Hot wheat cereal
English muffin, selected
    margarine and plum jam
Skim or low-fat milk
Coffee or tea

[1] Where margarine is indicated, use unsalted polyunsaturated margarine.

LUNCH
Chef's Salad with True
Italian Dressing* (make
Good Green Salad,* add-
ing strips of chicken, Swiss
cheese and lean beef)
Sesame Twists*
Cherry Cobbler*
Skim or low-fat milk
Coffee or tea

DINNER
Roast Lamb* with mint jelly
Mashed Potatoes*
Asparagus Polonaise*
Tomato Aspic*
Parkerhouse rolls with
selected margarine
Lemon Chiffon Pie*
Coffee or tea

DAY 3

BREAKFAST
Cantaloupe
Puffed wheat
Cinnamon toast
Skim or low-fat milk
Coffee or tea

LUNCH
Jellied Gazpacho*
Shrimp salad sandwich
Canned plums
Skim or low-fat milk
Coffee or tea

DINNER
Beef and Rice Skillet Dinner*
Zucchini*
Jellied Waldorf Salad*
Club rolls with selected
margarine
Apricot Skillet Cake*
Coffee or tea

DAY 4

BREAKFAST
Strawberries
Canadian bacon
Toast and selected margarine
Skim or low-fat milk
Coffee or tea

LUNCH
Broiled Fish Fillets with
Sesame*
Basque Potatoes*
Chinese Slaw*
Soft rolls with selected
margarine
Date and Nut Bars*
Skim or low-fat milk
Coffee or tea

DINNER
Lamb Stew*
Boiled Potatoes*
Perfection Salad*
Bread sticks with selected
margarine
Broiled Bananas with Sour
Cream*
Coffee or tea

SUMMER

DAY 1

BREAKFAST
Orange juice
Blueberry pancakes with
selected margarine and
syrup
Skim or low-fat milk
Coffee or tea

LUNCH
Salad: Cottage cheese and
fruits in season with Citrus
Honey Dressing*

Melba toast and selected
   margarine
Oatmeal Fudge Cookies*
Iced tea

DINNER
Broiled Lamb Chops*
Spaghetti with Eggplant
   Sauce*
Good Green Salad* with
   True Italian Dressing*
Pumpernickel bread with
   selected margarine
Yellow Cake* with California
   Orange Sauce*
Coffee or tea

DAY 2

BREAKFAST
Raspberries
Soft-cooked egg
Toast and selected margarine
Skim or low-fat milk
Coffee or tea

LUNCH
Sliced cold roast veal
Macaroni Salad, Italian
   Style*
Sliced tomatoes and
   cucumbers
Strawberry Snow*
Skim or low-fat milk
Coffee or tea

DINNER
Quick Gazpacho*
Baked Chicken with Grapes*
Really Good Rice*
Fruit salad: Fresh peaches
   and blueberries with Pink
   Poppyseed Dressing*

Thin rye crackers with
   selected margarine
Maple-Baked Pears*
Coffee or tea

DAY 3

BREAKFAST
Quarter honeydew
English muffin with peanut
   butter and grape jelly
Skim or low-fat milk
Coffee or tea

LUNCH
Jellied Orange Chicken
   Salad*
Poppyseed rolls and selected
   margarine
Vanilla yogurt with sliced
   fresh peaches
Coffee or tea

DINNER
Chili Pear Broil*
Armenian Ground Lamb
   Kabobs*
Mexican Style Corn*
Curried Rice*
Celery fans
Vanilla Trifle*
Coffee or tea

DAY 4

BREAKFAST
Corn flakes and strawberries
Toast, selected margarine and
   orange marmalade
Skim or low-fat milk
Coffee or tea

LUNCH
Hungarian Goulash*
Noodles*

Sliced tomatoes with Sweet
   Mayonnaise Dressing*
Banana
Skim or low-fat milk
Coffee or tea

DINNER

Baked Whole Fish in Foil*
Baked Potato*
Grapefruit and Mushroom
   Salad*
Cherry tomatoes
Bran muffins and selected
   margarine
Molded Summer Fruit*
Coffee or tea

FALL

DAY 1

BREAKFAST

Puffed wheat with sliced
   banana
Toast, selected margarine and
   grape jelly
Skim or low-fat milk
Coffee or tea

LUNCH

Tomato stuffed with chicken
   salad
Party-size rye bread and
   selected margarine
Honeydew Tropicale*
Skim or low-fat milk
Coffee or tea

DINNER

Spiced Garbanzos*
Apple-Stuffed Veal Rolls*
Poppyseed Noodles*
Good Green Salad* with
   Tomato Salad Dressing*
Cherry Pie*
Coffee or tea

DAY 2

BREAKFAST

Half grapefruit, broiled
One egg, scrambled
Toast, selected margarine
   and cherry preserves
Skim or low-fat milk
Coffee or tea

LUNCH

Halibut Steak Jardinière*
Really Good Rice*
Apple Crisp*
Skim or low-fat milk
Coffee or tea

DINNER

Old-Fashioned Stuffed
   Cabbage*
Mashed Turnips* and
   potatoes
Dilled Cucumber Slices*
Rye bread and selected
   margarine
Streusel Coffee Cake*
Coffee or tea

DAY 3

BREAKFAST

Unsweetened pineapple-
   grapefruit juice
French toast and honey
Skim or low-fat milk
Coffee or tea

LUNCH

Slim-line Beef Patties* on a
   bun with selected marga-
   rine and Sweet Catsup
   Sauce*
Potato Salad*
Radishes
Easy Apple-Noodle Bake*
Skim or low-fat milk
Coffee or tea

DINNER

Chicken Piccata*
Noodles* with selected
    margarine
Chinese-Style Cabbage*
Fruit salad: Pears, halved red
    grapes and oranges
Poppyseed Dressing*
Oatmeal Batter Bread* and
    selected margarine
Orange sherbet
Austrian Crescents*
Coffee or tea

DAY 4

BREAKFAST

Two tangerines
Pancakes, selected marga-
    rine and syrup
Skim or low-fat milk
Coffee or tea

LUNCH

Deviled egg
Old-Fashioned Macaroni
    Salad*
Sliced tomato
Fruit Juice Snow*
Skim or low-fat milk
Coffee or tea

DINNER

Oatmeal Meat Loaf
    Neapolitan*
Mashed Potatoes*
Italian-Style Green Beans*
Jellied Orange and Apple
    Salad (see Invent-Your-
    Own Jellied Fruit Salad*)
Hot garlic bread (made with
    selected margarine)
Canned pineapple rings
Almond Squares*
Coffee or tea

WINTER

DAY 1

BREAKFAST

Stewed apricots
Hot oatmeal
English muffins with
    selected margarine
Skim or low-fat milk
Coffee or tea

LUNCH

Tarragon-Broiled
    Hamburger*
Spanish Rice*
Cole slaw
Canned pears
Skim or low-fat milk
Coffee or tea

DINNER

Fish Steaks Provençal*
Boiled Potatoes* with marga-
    rine and parsley
Broccoli Florentine*
Cucumber slices in Basic
    French Dressing*
Poppyseed Batter Bread*
    with selected margarine
Buttermilk Lemon Sherbet*
Coffee or tea

DAY 2

BREAKFAST

Half grapefruit
Puffed rice
Toast with selected margarine
    and jam
Skim or low-fat milk
Coffee or tea

LUNCH

Sandwich: Swiss cheese on
    rye with selected marga-

rine, lettuce and Hot
  Mustard Sauce, Dijon
  Style*
Sliced tomato
Old-Fashioned Doughnut*
Skim or low-fat milk
Coffee or tea

DINNER
Chicken with Peaches*
Green Peas à la Française*
Golden Rice*
Good Green Salad*
Hot French bread and
  selected margarine
Canned Royal Anne cherries
Coffee or tea

DAY 3

BREAKFAST
Orange juice
Toast and peanut butter
Skim or low-fat milk
Coffee or tea

LUNCH
Beef-Vegetable Soup*
Onion Bread Rounds* with
  selected margarine
Pineapple Whip*
Butterscotch Brownies*
Skim or low-fat milk
Coffee or tea

DINNER
Roast Pork* with apple
  sauce
Spiced Red Cabbage*

Mashed Potatoes*
Dilled Cucumber Slices*
Popovers* with selected
  margarine
Banana Fruit Cups* with
  Spirited Syrup*
Coffee or tea

DAY 4

BREAKFAST
Stewed prunes
Cream of rice cereal
Toast with selected margarine
  and strawberry jam
Skim or low-fat milk
Coffee or tea

LUNCH
Sandwich: Chicken, sliced
  tomatoes, lettuce, selected
  margarine, Sweet Mayon-
  naise Dressing* on Good
  White Bread*
Pineapple Relish Mold*
Skim or low-fat milk
Coffee or tea

DINNER
Savory Meat Loaf*
Baked Potatoes*
Dilly Beans and Carrots*
Sesame Pears*
Celery, Radishes
Flaky Biscuits* with selected
  margarine
Angel Food Cake* with
  thawed frozen raspberries
Coffee or tea

CHAPTER 3

APPETIZERS, SOUPS AND RELISHES

CHAPTER 3

APPETIZERS, SOUPS AND RELISHES

Though the foods in this chapter are not served every day, they are part of every good cook's stock in trade.

When you entertain friends, it's nice to provide snacks (hors d'oeuvres) to accompany liquid refreshment. Try the appetizers included here.

Good soups have many functions. At company meals a homemade soup can set the stage for what's ahead. When the family dinner is a bit late, a mug of soup in the kitchen comforts Dad and the youngsters without destroying appetites. Hearty soups can serve as a lunch or supper, since many contain both meat and vegetables. Soup adds a pleasant hot touch to sandwich meals. Homemade beef, chicken or turkey broth on hand in the refrigerator or freezer is a quick and easy stepping stone to many delicious recipes.

Read on for other tasty mealtime accompaniments, pungent relishes and spicy fruit go-alongs. Ideal for company, they are also a real treat for "just the family."

PICKLED MUSHROOMS

1 lb. fresh mushrooms
1¼ cups cider vinegar
⅓ cup water
1 tablespoon instant minced onion
1½ teaspoons Morton Lite Salt mixture

½ teaspoon coarse-ground black pepper
2 bay leaves
6 to 8 celery leaves
2 sprigs parsley, or 1 tablespoon parsley flakes

Wash mushrooms, pat dry and trim off stem ends. Cut large mushrooms in half. Place in bowl. In a small saucepan, combine remaining ingredients. Bring to a boil; reduce heat and simmer for 5 minutes. Pour over mushrooms; cool. Spoon mushrooms and marinade into a 1-quart jar with a tight cover. Refrigerate 24 hours before serving. Makes 1 quart.

Per Recipe

Calories	410	Sodium	1783 mg.
Carbohydrate	93 Gm.	Potassium	4200 mg.
Protein	19 Gm.	Cholesterol	0
Fat	3 Gm.		

MARINATED ARTICHOKE HEARTS

2 packages (9 oz. each) frozen artichoke hearts
¾ cup vegetable oil
⅓ cup tarragon vinegar
2 tablespoons finely chopped parsley

1 tablespoon finely chopped onion
1 teaspoon dry mustard
½ teaspoon Morton Lite Salt mixture
¼ teaspoon pepper
1 clove garlic, minced

Cook artichoke hearts following package directions for minimum cooking period, crisp-tender. Drain. Meanwhile, mix remaining ingredients in medium bowl. Add artichoke hearts and toss. Cover and refrigerate overnight. Serve chilled. (Artichokes may also be heated in the marinade and served from a fondue pot or chafing dish held over low heat.) Serve with wooden picks. Makes about 60, enough for 10.

Per Serving

Calories	161	Sodium	67 mg.
Carbohydrate	2 Gm.	Potassium	87 mg.
Protein	trace	Cholesterol	0
Fat	17 Gm.		

VEGETABLE ANTIPASTO

⅔ cup white vinegar
⅔ cup vegetable oil
2 tablespoons instant minced onion
1 teaspoon Italian seasoning
1 teaspoon Morton Lite Salt mixture
1 teaspoon sugar
¼ teaspoon instant minced garlic

⅛ teaspoon coarse-ground black pepper
1 can (14 oz.) artichoke hearts, drained and halved
1 can (6 to 8 oz.) sliced mushrooms, drained
1 can (7¼ oz.) baby carrots, drained
1 jar (2½ oz.) pitted ripe olives, drained

In a small saucepan, combine vinegar, oil and seasonings. Bring to boiling point. Cool slightly. Mix vegetables in a bowl. Add marinade and toss to coat. Cover and refrigerate at least 12 hours, or overnight. Makes 1 quart.

Per Recipe

Calories	1086	Sodium	2513 mg.
Carbohydrate	188 Gm.	Potassium	4500 mg.
Protein	29 Gm.	Cholesterol	0
Fat	34 Gm.		

SPICED GARBANZOS

1 tablespoon instant minced
onion
1 tablespoon water
1 can (1 lb. 4 oz.) chick peas
(garbanzos), drained

¼ teaspoon pepper
⅛ teaspoon Morton Lite Salt
mixture
Dash garlic powder

In a small bowl, mix onion with water and let stand 10 minutes. Add remaining ingredients; toss gently. Chill. Makes 2 cups.

Per Recipe

Calories	2283	Sodium	346 mg.
Carbohydrate	403 Gm.	Potassium	250 mg.
Protein	122 Gm.	Cholesterol	0
Fat	28 Gm.		

RAW VEGETABLE MEDLEY

1 small head cauliflower
2 medium carrots
1 bunch radishes
2 bunches green onions

1 medium zucchini
3 stalks celery
Mustard Dill Dip
Celery Seed Dip

Cut cauliflower into flowerets. Wash and drain on paper towel. Peel carrots and slice thin on the diagonal. Rinse and drain. Trim radishes and wash well. Make into roses and crisp in ice water. Trim off root ends of green onions and peel off outer layer. Trim so 2 inches of green remain. Rinse in cold water. Trim off ends of zucchini and scrub under cold water. Cut in half lengthwise, then cut into strips about ½ inch square and 3 inches long. Crisp in ice water. Trim ends from celery and cut each stalk into half-inch strips about 3 inches long. Rinse and drain. Arrange all these vegetables on a platter in a pleasing design, garnishing if desired with parsley or curly endive. Serve with Mustard Dill Dip and Celery Seed Dip. Serves 10.

Per Serving

Calories	21	Sodium	31 mg.
Carbohydrate	5 Gm.	Potassium	100 mg.
Protein	1 Gm.	Cholesterol	0
Fat	trace		

MUSTARD DILL DIP

1 cup dairy sour cream
1 teaspoon prepared mustard
1 teaspoon dill weed

½ teaspoon Morton Lite Salt mixture
½ teaspoon prepared horseradish (optional)

Combine all ingredients in small bowl, stirring until well mixed. Chill at least 6 hours or overnight. Makes 1 cup.

Per Recipe

Calories	458	Sodium	711 mg.
Carbohydrate	8 Gm.	Potassium	800 mg.
Protein	7 Gm.	Cholesterol	152 mg.
Fat	44 Gm.		

CELERY SEED DIP

1 cup dairy sour cream
1 teaspoon celery seed

½ teaspoon Morton Lite Salt mixture
½ teaspoon dry mustard

Combine all ingredients and stir until well mixed. Chill at least 6 hours or overnight. Makes 1 cup.

Per Recipe

Calories	454	Sodium	646 mg.
Carbohydrate	8 Gm.	Potassium	*
Protein	7 Gm.	Cholesterol	152 mg.
Fat	43 Gm.		

* Data not available.

AVOCADO DIP

2 tablespoons instant minced onion
2 tablespoons water
2 ripe avocados, peeled and pitted
¼ cup diced tomato
¼ cup mayonnaise
3 tablespoons lemon juice
2 teaspoons chili powder
1¼ teaspoons Morton Lite Salt mixture
½ teaspoon coarse-ground black pepper
¼ teaspoon garlic powder

Mix onion with water and let stand 10 minutes. Mash avocado in small mixing bowl. Add onion along with remaining ingredients; mix well. Serve with vegetable relishes. Makes about 2 cups.

Per Recipe

Calories	1031	Sodium	1402 mg.
Carbohydrate	31 Gm.	Potassium	2800 mg.
Protein	9 Gm.	Cholesterol	40 mg.
Fat	102 Gm.		

BAKED STUFFED MUSHROOMS

8 to 10 large fresh mushrooms
⅓ cup dry bread crumbs
2 tablespoons chopped walnuts
2 teaspoons dry minced chives
1 teaspoon parsley flakes
½ teaspoon paprika
½ teaspoon Morton Lite Salt mixture
⅛ teaspoon pepper
2 tablespoons half-and-half
Vegetable oil

Wash mushrooms, trim stems, then remove stems. Lay caps aside and chop stems. Combine the chopped stems with bread crumbs, walnuts, chives, parsley, paprika, salt and pepper. Add half-and-half; toss with a fork to moisten all ingredients. Brush mushroom caps inside and out with vegetable oil. Fill each mushroom cap with crumb mixture. Drizzle with vegetable oil, using about ⅛ teaspoon for each mushroom. Place in a greased 9-inch-square pan. Bake at 400° for 20 minutes, or until mushroom caps are just tender and crumb mixture is lightly browned. Serve immediately. Serves 4.

Calories	108	Sodium	202 mg.
Carbohydrate	9 Gm.	Potassium	425 mg.
Protein	3 Gm.	Cholesterol	6 mg.
Fat	7 Gm.		

HOMEMADE POPCORN

3 tablespoons vegetable oil
½ cup popcorn
¼ cup melted unsalted polyun-
saturated margarine

½ teaspoon Morton Lite Salt mixture

Place oil in a heavy 4-quart saucepan or deep-fryer. Add 1 kernel popcorn and place over medium high heat. When kernel pops, remove it and add remaining popcorn. Stir to mix popcorn and oil. Place cover on pan, leaving a small air space at the edge of the cover to let steam escape. Shake pan frequently until popping stops. Near the end of the popping, remove cover completely and stir until the last few kernels pop. Remove from heat. Add margarine and salt and toss well. Turn into a warm bowl and serve immediately. Makes about 3 quarts.

Per Recipe

Calories	1118	Sodium	558 mg.
Carbohydrate	61 Gm.	Potassium	740 mg.
Protein	10 Gm.	Cholesterol	0
Fat	95 Gm.		

QUICK GAZPACHO

1 cup water
1 lb. fresh tomatoes, peeled and diced
1 cucumber, peeled and sliced
¼ cup mixed vegetable flakes
1 tablespoon onion powder
¼ teaspoon garlic powder
¼ teaspoon Morton Lite Salt mixture

⅛ teaspoon ground red pepper
¼ cup olive or vegetable oil
2 tablespoons wine vinegar

* * *

Croutons, diced tomato and cucumber (optional)

In jar of electric blender, combine all ingredients except oil and vinegar. Cover and blend until almost smooth. Stir in oil and vinegar. Chill well. Serve in bowls and, if desired, garnish with croutons, diced tomato and cucumber. Serves 4.

Per Serving

Calories	215	Sodium	89 mg.
Carbohydrate	21 Gm.	Potassium	368 mg.
Protein	3 Gm.	Cholesterol	0
Fat	14 Gm.		

POTATO SOUP

2 tablespoons unsalted polyunsaturated margarine
1 large onion, finely chopped
5 large potatoes, peeled and cut in small pieces

1 cup water
3 cups milk
2 teaspoons Morton Lite Salt mixture
Pepper to taste

Heat margarine in large saucepan. Add onion and cook until tender. Add potatoes and water; bring to boil and boil gently for 15 minutes, or until potatoes are tender. Mash the mixture. Gradually stir in milk and seasonings. Heat slowly to serving temperature, stirring occasionally to prevent sticking. Makes 6 cups.

Per Cup Serving

Calories	186	Sodium	432 mg.
Carbohydrate	21 Gm.	Potassium	988 mg.
Protein	6 Gm.	Cholesterol	13 mg.
Fat	8 Gm.		

BEEF-VEGETABLE SOUP

1 lb. beef short ribs
7 cups water
2 teaspoons Morton Lite Salt mixture
⅛ teaspoon pepper
2 cups tomatoes, peeled and diced (fresh or canned)

1 cup diced potatoes
¾ cup thin-sliced carrots
½ cup sliced onions
3 cups other mixed vegetables (peas, cabbage, celery, green beans, green pepper, corn)

The day before you plan to serve this soup combine beef, water and salt in a large saucepan. Bring to a boil; cover and simmer until meat can be easily removed from bones. Remove meat to cutting board. Discard bones and visible fat. Return to broth and chill overnight. Next day, lift off and discard fat layer. Reheat, adding remaining ingredients; cover and cook for 35 minutes, or until all vegetables are tender. (If any of the vegetables are canned or cooked, add them during the last 5 minutes of cooking time.) Taste and adjust seasoning. Makes 10 cups.

Per Cup Serving

Calories	99	Sodium	244 mg.
Carbohydrate	9 Gm.	Potassium	440 mg.
Protein	5 Gm.	Cholesterol	15 mg.
Fat	5 Gm.		

BEEF NOODLE SOUP

1¼ lbs. beef short ribs
1 tablespoon Morton Lite Salt mixture
6 cups water

1 cup celery with leaves, chopped
4 oz. uncooked noodles

The day before you are planning to serve this soup, place beef, salt, and water in a large saucepan. Bring to a boil, reduce heat, and simmer, covered, about 2 hours, or until meat is tender. Remove beef to cutting board. Discard bones and visible fat. Cut meat into small pieces. Return meat to broth and refrigerate. Next day, lift off and discard fat layer. Reheat soup to boiling. Add celery; cover and simmer for 10 minutes. Stir in noodles. Cover and simmer about 10 minutes, or until noodles are tender. Makes 6 cups.

Per Cup Serving

Calories	197	Sodium	588 mg.
Carbohydrate	14 Gm.	Potassium	861 mg.
Protein	10 Gm.	Cholesterol	89 mg.
Fat	11 Gm.		

BEAN CHOWDER

¾ cup dry navy beans
4 cups water
1½ teaspoons Morton Lite Salt mixture
¾ cup diced potato
½ cup chopped onion

1½ teaspoons flour
1 tablespoon unsalted polyunsaturated margarine
¾ cup canned tomatoes
⅓ cup minced green pepper
1½ cups milk

The day before, wash and pick over beans. Place in saucepan with water, bring to a boil, cook for 2 minutes, remove from heat and let stand, covered, overnight. Next day, add salt and bring to a boil. Cover and boil until almost done (about 1 hour). Add potato and onion; cook for 30 minutes more. Combine flour with margarine and stir in. Add tomatoes and green pepper. Cook over low heat for 10 minutes, stirring constantly until thickened, then occasionally to prevent scorching. Stir in milk and heat to serving temperature. Makes 4½ cups.

Calories	248	Sodium	478 mg.
Carbohydrate	36 Gm.	Potassium	1027 mg.
Protein	13 Gm.	Cholesterol	9 mg.
Fat	6 Gm.		

NEW ENGLAND FISH CHOWDER

½ cup onion flakes
3⅓ cups water
2 tablespoons vegetable oil
2 cups sliced potatoes
¼ cup mixed vegetable flakes
2 teaspoons Morton Lite Salt mixture
½ teaspoon garlic powder
¼ teaspoon ground black pepper

2 cups milk
2 tablespoons flour
2 small bay leaves
2 lbs. frozen fish fillets, thawed and cut in chunks

* * *

1½ teaspoons parsley flakes
½ teaspoon paprika

Let onion flakes stand in ⅓ cup of the water for 10 minutes. In a large saucepan, heat oil. Add onion and sauté for 5 minutes. Remove from heat. Add remaining 3 cups of water, potatoes, vegetable flakes, salt, garlic powder and black pepper. Bring to a boil. Reduce heat; cover and simmer for 15 minutes, or until potatoes are almost tender. Combine milk and flour. Slowly stir into saucepan; add bay leaves and fish. Simmer, without boiling, for 15 minutes, or just until fish flakes easily with a fork. Remove bay leaves. Ladle into bowls, sprinkling each serving with parsley and paprika. Makes 10 cups.

Per Cup Serving

Calories	405	Sodium	363 mg.
Carbohydrate	67 Gm.	Potassium	501 mg.
Protein	25 Gm.	Cholesterol	68 mg.
Fat	5 Gm.		

BROTH FROM LEFTOVERS

When you have beef roast left over from a company meal, don't discard the rack. Put the bones, along with the meat clinging to them, into a soup kettle and add about a quart of water and, if you like, a peeled onion and a few celery tops. Bring to a boil, reduce heat and simmer gently for 2 hours. Turn the pieces of meat-and-bones from time to time. Strain the resulting broth into a bowl and refrigerate. Next day, lift off and discard the fat layer. The broth will probably have some sediment at the bottom which can be used for flavoring gravies. The rest may be used for beef broth.

Making excellent turkey broth is an easy task. After you have removed most of the meat from the carcass, break it into pieces and put it into the soup kettle. You may also add all the skin and any meaty pieces your family does not plan to eat. Onion and celery may be added for flavor. Simmer for 2 to 3 hours, turning bones occasionally. Remove bones, taking off any salvageable meat. Strain the broth into a bowl. Chill. The next day remove the fat layer. The broth may be frozen or used within 3 days. A good quick soup may be had by bringing broth to a boil, adding any reserved meat and fine noodles or rice. Taste, and add Morton Lite Salt mixture and pepper as needed. The carcass of a 20-pound turkey will make about 1½ quarts of flavorful broth.

Even if your family enjoys eating chicken breasts and legs only, it is always cheaper to buy whole chickens cut up. Use the parts you like for frying or broiling; make a soup from the remainder. Place necks, wing tips, backs and giblets in a saucepan and cover with water. Season as desired. Simmer for 2 hours. Strain the broth, chill, remove fat and use broth as desired within 3 days, or freeze for a longer period.

(See also Simmered Chicken, page 72.)

CHICKEN AND MUSHROOM BROTH

1 quart homemade chicken broth
½ teaspoon Morton Lite Salt mixture
1 carrot, thinly sliced

¼ lb. fresh mushrooms
¼ lb. spinach, washed and chopped
1 tomato, peeled and diced

In a medium saucepan, combine broth, salt and carrot. Bring to a boil. Reduce heat, cover and simmer for 5 to 8 minutes. Rinse mushrooms and pat dry. Trim off stem ends and slice. Add to broth along with spinach and tomato. Cover and simmer for 5 minutes. Makes 6 cups.

Per Cup Serving

Calories	30	Sodium	168 mg.
Carbohydrate	3 Gm.	Potassium	359 mg.
Protein	3 Gm.	Cholesterol	0
Fat	1 Gm.		

CHICKEN GUMBO

4 cups homemade chicken broth
½ cup canned or cooked tomatoes
½ cup thin sliced green pepper
½ cup thin sliced onion
1 teaspoon Morton Lite Salt mixture

1 tablespoon minced parsley
2 cups cooked, diced chicken
1 package (10 oz.) frozen okra, cut up
½ cup cooked rice
½ cup cooked corn

Heat chicken broth, adding tomatoes, green pepper, onion, salt and parsley. Bring to a boil, reduce heat and simmer about 20 minutes, or until onion and pepper are tender. Add chicken and okra; cook 5 minutes longer. Add rice and corn and heat through. Makes 2 quarts.

Per Cup Serving

Calories	106	Sodium	199 mg.
Carbohydrates	12 Gm.	Potassium	414 mg.
Protein	10 Gm.	Cholesterol	24 mg.
Fat	3 Gm.		

HOMEMADE BEEF BROTH

3 lbs. soup bones
1 lb. beef stew meat, cut up
(optional)
3 quarts water
1 tablespoon Morton Lite
Salt mixture
⅓ cup celery, chopped

⅓ cup carrots, diced
⅓ cup onion, chopped
2 sprigs parsley, chopped
5 whole cloves
1 bay leaf
Other seasonings as desired

If you buy your meat at a supermarket, the butcher may need advance notice to provide you with soup bones, which should be sawed into pieces to expose more marrow. You may also use bones cut from a roast—even leftover bones. Cut off all the meat from the bones before cooking. A good stock may be made using nothing except beef stew meat, although this is more expensive. Oil the bottom of a stew pot or Dutch oven, add meat and brown well. (This step insures a rich brown color for the stock.) Then cover bones and browned meat with water. Add salt and remaining ingredients. Cover and simmer for 3½ to 4 hours. (In place of some of the water, you can use vegetable liquids from cooking.) Taste the stock and adjust seasonings. At this point, if you have used stew meat, the meat should be removed for use in croquettes, hash, etc. Strain the remaining broth into a bowl. Refrigerate overnight. Next day, lift off and discard the fat layer. Use broth as desired. It should be heated to boiling at least every other day to prevent spoilage, or used within 3 days, or frozen. Makes 2 quarts.

Per Cup Serving

Calories	54	Sodium	345 mg.
Carbohydrate	1 Gm.	Potassium	624 mg.
Protein	2 Gm.	Cholesterol	6 mg.
Fat	4 Gm.		

Beef Soup: After straining the broth you can save all the cooked vegetables and meat and, after overnight storage to remove fat, heat these foods in some of the broth for a fine soup. It may be seasoned with thyme, garlic, nutmeg, cloves, sage, poultry seasoning, Tabasco sauce or cayenne. *Bouillon:* To clarify the broth to make bouillon, follow this procedure. To each quart of cold stock add the beaten white and crushed shell of 1 egg. Bring slowly to a boil, stirring constantly. Boil about 5 minutes. Add ½ cup of cold water and let stand for 10 minutes. Strain through cheesecloth.

Note: Nutrients will vary with cut of beef and the care in skimming off fat.

FRENCH ONION SOUP

5 cups thin sliced sweet Spanish onions
¼ cup unsalted polyunsaturated margarine
3 tablespoons flour
2 quarts homemade chicken or beef broth

Morton Lite Salt mixture to taste
¼ teaspoon white pepper

* * *

Cognac (optional)

Onions may be sliced to form rings or the circles may be cut into quarters for easier eating. In a heavy saucepan or Dutch oven, melt margarine. Add onions and toss lightly until coated with margarine. Reduce heat, cover and cook until wilted and tender (10 to 15 minutes). For a dark onion soup, allow onions to brown a little. Remove cover. Add flour and stir to mix well. Cook for 3 minutes over low heat. Add broth. (Beef broth is traditional, but chicken broth produces a soup with an unusually delicious flavor.) Taste, and add salt as desired. Add pepper. Reduce heat to simmer and cover; cook gently for 1 hour to develop flavor. Makes 2 quarts.

To Freeze: The cooled soup may be placed in appropriate containers and frozen. The soup should be thawed in the refrigerator for a full day, then reheated very slowly. A little cognac (¼ cup for half the recipe) may be added just before serving.

Per Cup Serving

Calories	135	Sodium	139 mg.
Carbohydrate	14 Gm.	Potassium	44 mg.
Protein	6 Gm.	Cholesterol	3 mg.
Fat	7 Gm.		

DILLED CUCUMBER SLICES

2 cucumbers
½ teaspoon Morton Lite Salt mixture
⅛ teaspoon coarse ground black pepper

2 teaspoons snipped fresh dill or 1 teaspoon dill weed
¼ cup vinegar

Wash and peel cucumbers and cut into very thin slices. Arrange in a bowl, sprinkling each layer with salt, pepper and dill. Pour vinegar over all. Cover and chill at least 2 hours. Serve with pierced spoon, or drain well. Slices may be used to top hamburgers in the buns in place of pickles. Makes 6 or more servings.

Per Serving

Calories	7	Sodium	94 mg.
Carbohydrate	2 Gm.	Potassium	141 mg.
Protein	trace	Cholesterol	0
Fat	trace		

ONION AND RED PEPPER RELISH

1 lb. sweet Spanish onions
1½ lbs. sweet red peppers
Boiling water
1 cup cider vinegar

½ cup sugar
2½ teaspoons Morton Lite Salt mixture

Peel onions and cut into small sections to make about 1 quart. Remove seeds, stems and any green spots from red peppers and cut into strips. Grind onions and peppers, using coarse blade of food chopper. Cover with boiling water and let stand 5 minutes. Drain in strainer. Combine onion and pepper with remaining ingredients in saucepan. Bring to a boil and simmer for 20 minutes. Cool, then store covered in the refrigerator. Makes about 3 cups.

Per Recipe

Calories	776	Sodium	2911 mg.
Carbohydrate	193 Gm.	Potassium	3640 mg.
Protein	17 Gm.	Cholesterol	0
Fat	2 Gm.		

PATIO CORN RELISH

1½ teaspoons dry mustard
1½ teaspoons warm water
4 ears corn, uncooked
1½ cups water
¾ cup cider vinegar
⅓ cup sugar
1¼ teaspoons Morton Lite
    Salt mixture

½ teaspoon celery seed
½ teaspoon ground turmeric
2 cups shredded cabbage
½ cup onion flakes
¼ cup sweet pepper flakes
¼ cup diced pimiento

Combine mustard with water and let stand for 10 minutes to develop flavor. Meanwhile, cut kernels from corn to make about 2¾ cups. Set aside. In a medium saucepan, combine mustard with 1½ cups of water, vinegar, sugar, salt, celery seed and turmeric. Bring to boil. Add cabbage, onion and sweet pepper flakes plus the reserved corn. Reduce heat to simmer. Cook, covered, for 25 minutes, stirring occasionally. Stir in pimiento and cook 5 minutes longer. May be spooned into hot sterile jars and sealed immediately, or stored in the refrigerator. Makes 2½ pints.

Per Recipe

Calories	931	Sodium	1558 mg.
Carbohydrate	217 Gm.	Potassium	4434 mg.
Protein	21 Gm.	Cholesterol	0 mg.
Fat	6 Gm.		

SPICED BROILED ORANGE BOATS

2 medium-size oranges
½ teaspoon cinnamon

½ teaspoon mace

Cut oranges in half crosswise. Remove seeds and, with small sharp knife, loosen sections. Sprinkle each half with a little of the cinnamon and mace. Broil for 7 minutes, or until hot and lightly browned. Serve with meat, fish, or poultry as appetizer-relish. Serves 4.

Per Serving

Calories	36	Sodium	1 mg.
Carbohydrate	9 Gm.	Potassium	100 mg.
Protein	trace	Cholesterol	0
Fat	trace		

CURRIED FRUIT APPETIZER

¼ cup chopped onion
1 clove garlic, minced
½ teaspoon Morton Lite Salt mixture
2½ teaspoons curry powder
½ teaspoon ginger
½ teaspoon dry mustard
¼ teaspoon pepper

2 tablespoons vinegar
1 tablespoon lemon juice
2 teaspoons honey
¼ cup tomato juice
2 apples, cored and cut in cubes
2 pears, cored and cut in cubes
1½ cups halved, seeded grapes
6 bananas

In a large saucepan, mix onion, garlic, salt, spices, vinegar, lemon juice, honey and tomato juice. Place over low heat, cover and simmer for 15 minutes. Cool. In a large bowl, combine apples, pears and grapes. Just before serving, slice bananas and mix in, then toss with curry dressing and serve. Makes 6 servings.

Per Serving

Calories	238	Sodium	121 mg.
Carbohydrate	57 Gm.	Potassium	156 mg.
Protein	3 Gm.	Cholesterol	0
Fat	1 Gm.		

CHILI PEAR BROIL

3 pears
2 tablespoons unsalted polyunsaturated margarine
2 tablespoons honey
Dash nutmeg

½ teaspoon chili powder
¼ teaspoon Morton Lite Salt mixture
Dash pepper

Cut pears in half and remove cores. Arrange, cut side up, on broiling rack. Mix remaining ingredients and brush over pears. Set broiling rack so pears are about 6 inches from heat. Broil for 10 to 12 minutes, brushing with sauce occasionally. Serve with meat. Serves 6.

Per Serving

Calories	118	Sodium	49 mg.
Carbohydrate	21 Gm.	Potassium	188 mg.
Protein	trace	Cholesterol	0
Fat	4 Gm.		

SESAME PEARS

3 ripe pears
Lemon juice
2 tablespoons sugar
½ cup bread crumbs

2 tablespoons unsalted polyunsaturated margarine, melted
2 teaspoons sesame seeds

Wash the pears. Cut them in half lengthwise and core. Brush cut surfaces with lemon juice and sprinkle each with 1 teaspoon of sugar. Broil, cut side up, 6 inches from heat source, about 8 minutes. Meantime combine bread crumbs, margarine and sesame seeds. Sprinkle over pears and broil for 2 to 3 minutes more, or until lightly browned. Nice with chicken. Serves 6.

Per Serving

Calories	174	Sodium	62 mg.
Carbohydrate	26 Gm.	Potassium	136 mg.
Protein	3 Gm.	Cholesterol	6 mg.
Fat	8 Gm.		

CRANBERRY-ORANGE RELISH

1 lb. (4 cups) cranberries
2 small oranges, quartered and seeded

1½ cups sugar

Wash and drain cranberries. Put cranberries and oranges through coarse blade of food chopper. Stir in sugar; chill. Makes 3 cups.

Note: Mixture may be put into suitable containers and frozen for future use. Allow to thaw in refrigerator for 24 hours before serving.

Per Recipe

Calories	1437	Sodium	11 mg.
Carbohydrate	366 Gm.	Potassium	760 mg.
Protein	4 Gm.	Cholesterol	0
Fat	3 Gm.		

HARVEST RELISH

1 lb. (4 cups) cranberries	2 cups sugar
2 small oranges, quartered and seeded	1 stalk celery, diced
	¼ cup chopped nuts

Wash and drain cranberries. Grind cranberries and oranges, using coarse blade of food chopper. Stir in sugar, celery and chopped nuts. Chill for several hours to blend flavors. Makes 1 quart.

Per Recipe

Calories	2066	Sodium	272 mg.
Carbohydrate	474 Gm.	Potassium	900 mg.
Protein	10 Gm.	Cholesterol	0
Fat	25 Gm.		

CHAPTER 4

MAIN DISHES

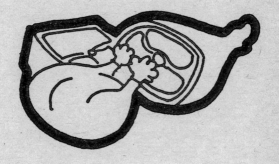

CHAPTER 4

MAIN DISHES

The chief function of main dishes, nutritionally speaking, is to provide protein for the body. Meat, poultry and fish also contain significant amounts of vitamins and minerals, at least one of which (B_{12}) is found only in animal protein.

In recent years we have become aware that meat also contains fat, both saturated and unsaturated.

The leaner cuts of beef—those which do not have a large amount of fat marbled throughout the lean—may be a wiser choice than an elegant filet mignon. Since pork is similar to beef in fattiness, it is best to cook it by dry-heat methods (below). Generally, most of the fat of lamb is easy to trim away. Veal is naturally low in fat. White fish is also lean by nature. Poultry products contain fat, but it is mostly under the skin and is easy to avoid.

If you wish to avoid saturated fat in cooking, choose dry-heat methods—roasting or broiling. Much fat drips away during cooking and, unless you make a gravy with it, is not served. If you stew meat, do it the day before you plan to serve it. Put it in a bowl in the refrigerator overnight; next day, lift off the layer of solid fat which forms on top. Reheat. You'll never miss the calories that were skimmed off!

Poaching or braising also releases fat from meat and poultry, although this fat passes into the cooking liquid.

Charcoal cooking is just like other forms of broiling and roasting. It reduces the fat in the meat while it adds a distinctive flavor of its own. This book does not include timetables for charcoal broiling since such times are difficult to predict. The heat of the fire and the amount of wind outdoors enter into how fast the meat cooks.

If you want to charcoal broil, let the coals burn until they are "white hot," covered with a light gray ash. Then put the meat on a grill over them. The broiling times given in this chapter will be the minimum times it takes the meat to be done through. If there is any breeze you will need more time. To test, cut into the meat and judge its pinkness.

A creative cook tries a new main dish at least once a month. (Or perhaps she knows how to make three hundred main dishes so her family is never bored.) The recipes which follow will give you a good running start!

Meat

TARRAGON-BROILED HAMBURGERS

1 lb. ground lean beef
¼ cup fresh lemon juice
¼ cup unsalted polyunsaturated margarine, melted

½ teaspoon tarragon leaves
½ teaspoon Morton Lite Salt mixture

Shape meat into 4 equal patties. Blend remaining ingredients. Brush over both sides of burgers. Broil for 6 to 7 minutes on one side. Turn, baste and broil for 3 minutes, or until meat has browned. Makes 4 patties.

Per Serving

Calories	216	Sodium	180 mg.
Carbohydrate	1 Gm.	Potassium	583 mg.
Protein	26 Gm.	Cholesterol	77 mg.
Fat	12 Gm.		

SLIM-LINE BEEF PATTIES

½ teaspoon dry mustard
1 tablespoon warm water
1 lb. ground lean beef
1 cup finely diced fresh
  mushrooms
1 cup finely chopped peeled
  tomato, drained

2 teaspoons instant minced onion
½ teaspoon Morton Lite Salt
  mixture
¼ teaspoon pepper
⅛ teaspoon garlic powder

Mix mustard with 1 tablespoon of warm water and let
stand for 10 minutes to develop flavor. Combine mustard
with remaining ingredients; mix well. Shape into 4 patties.
Broil for 6 to 7 minutes; turn and brown second side,
about 3 minutes. Makes 4 patties.

Per Serving

Calories	160	Sodium	192 mg.
Carbohydrate	4 Gm.	Potassium	820 mg.
Protein	27 Gm.	Cholesterol	77 mg.
Fat	4 Gm.		

OATMEAL MEAT LOAF NEAPOLITAN

2 lbs. ground lean beef
1 cup quick-cooking oatmeal
1 can (8 oz.) tomato sauce
½ cup chopped onion
½ cup chopped green pepper
2 lightly beaten eggs

1½ teaspoons Morton Lite
  Salt mixture
¼ teaspoon crushed rosemary
¼ teaspoon crushed oregano
¼ teaspoon crushed basil

In a large bowl, mix all ingredients well. Pack into 9″
×5″ ×3″ loaf pan, handling gently. Bake at 400° for
1 hour, 15 minutes or until top is browned. Drain fat.
Let stand in pan for 5 minutes; slice. Makes 8 servings.

Per Serving

Calories	221	Sodium	391 mg.
Carbohydrate	11 Gm.	Potassium	816 mg.
Protein	30 Gm.	Cholesterol	145 mg.
Fat	6 Gm.		

SAVORY MEAT LOAF

1 egg, lightly beaten
¾ teaspoon Morton Lite Salt mixture
⅛ teaspoon pepper
¾ cup cooked or canned tomatoes, cut up, with liquid

¾ cup soft bread cubes
¼ cup finely chopped celery with leaves
¼ cup minced parsley
⅓ cup finely chopped onion
1½ lbs. lean ground beef
¼ lb. bulk pork sausage

In a large bowl, blend ingredients together in order given. Pack into 9″ × 5″ × 3″ loaf pan. Bake at 350° for 1½ hours. Drain fat. Let stand for 5 minutes; slice. Makes 8 slices.

For a Meat Loaf with Crusty Sides: Choose a shallow baking pan (13″ × 9″ × 2″, for example). Press, knead and pat meat into a long narrow loaf shape. Bake as above. Use two pancake turners to lift onto platter.

Per Slice

Calories	202	Sodium	172 mg.
Carbohydrate	4 Gm.	Potassium	686 mg.
Protein	23 Gm.	Cholesterol	102 mg.
Fat	10 Gm.		

BEEF AND RICE SKILLET DINNER

2 tablespoons vegetable oil
1 lb. lean stewing beef, cut in 1-inch cubes
3 cups water
1 can (6 oz.) tomato paste
1 cup uncooked rice (not pre-cooked variety)

1 medium onion, cut in half slices
1 large tomato, peeled and cut in half slices
1½ teaspoons Morton Lite Salt mixture
¾ teaspoon crushed red pepper

Heat oil in large skillet over medium heat. Add beef; brown on all sides, turning as needed. Add 1 cup of water. Cover and simmer for 45 minutes, or until meat is tender. Add remaining 2 cups of water; gradually stir in tomato paste. Add rice, onion, tomato, salt and pepper.

Bring to boil. Cover; reduce heat and simmer, stirring occasionally, for 25 minutes, or until rice is tender. Makes 5 servings.

Per Serving

Calories	425	Sodium	405 mg.
Carbohydrate	31 Gm.	Potassium	859 mg.
Protein	33 Gm.	Cholesterol	59 mg.
Fat	18 Gm.		

ONION TOPPED BEEF BAKE

1 medium sweet Spanish onion
1 tablespoon vegetable oil
2 lbs. lean ground beef
2 teaspoons Morton Lite Salt mixture
½ teaspoon pepper
½ teaspoon thyme
1 green pepper, cleaned and diced
3 medium potatoes
1 can (15 oz.) tomato sauce
Parsley, for garnish

Peel and thinly slice onion. Sauté in vegetable oil until just tender. Remove to absorbent paper. Brown ground beef slowly in skillet; drain. Blend in salt, pepper and thyme. Add green pepper. Peel and thinly slice potatoes. Place half of potato slices on bottom of 2½-quart buttered casserole. Top with half the ground beef mixture. Repeat layers. Top with onion rings. Pour tomato sauce over all. Cover and bake at 350° for 1 hour and 15 minutes, or until potatoes and onions are tender. Serve garnished with parsley. Makes 6 servings.

Per Serving

Calories	291	Sodium	761 mg.
Carbohydrate	19 Gm.	Potassium	1356 mg.
Protein	38 Gm.	Cholesterol	103 mg.
Fat	7 Gm.		

STIFADO (Greek Beef Stew)

3 tablespoons vegetable oil
2½ lbs. lean boneless beef stew meat, cut in 2-inch cubes
½ cup onion flakes
2¼ cups water
3 tablespoons flour
1 can (6 oz.) tomato paste
¼ cup cider vinegar

1 stick (4-inch) cinnamon, broken in half, or ¾ teaspoon ground cinnamon
4 whole cloves
2 teaspoons Morton Lite Salt mixture
½ teaspoon pepper

In Dutch oven or large heavy saucepan, heat oil. Add beef and brown well on all sides. Meantime, let onion flakes stand in ¼ cup of water for 10 minutes. Add to meat and cook for 3 minutes. Stir in flour; cook 2 minutes longer. Pour in remaining 2 cups of water along with remaining ingredients. Bring to boil. Cover; reduce heat and simmer for 1½ hours, or until meat is tender. Remove cinnamon stick and cloves before serving. Makes 6 servings.

Per Serving

Calories	327	Sodium	420 mg.
Carbohydrate	12 Gm.	Potassium	1250 mg.
Protein	38 Gm.	Cholesterol	78 mg.
Fat	12 Gm.		

BEEF CARBONNADE

½ cup onion flakes
⅓ cup water
2½ lbs. lean boneless beef stew meat, cut in 2-inch cubes
⅓ cup flour
¼ cup vegetable oil
1 can (12 oz.) beer

2 teaspoons Morton Lite Salt mixture
¼ teaspoon garlic powder
¼ teaspoon ground nutmeg
¼ teaspoon powdered thyme
¼ teaspoon pepper

Mix onion flakes and water and let stand for 10 minutes. Place beef in plastic bag with flour and shake to coat beef well. In a Dutch oven or large heavy skillet, heat oil. Add beef and brown on all sides. Add onion; sauté for 5 minutes. Stir in remaining ingredients. Cover; reduce heat and simmer for 1½ hours, or until meat is tender. Makes 6 servings.

Per Serving

Calories	357	Sodium	410 mg.
Carbohydrate	10 Gm.	Potassium	950 mg.
Protein	37 Gm.	Cholesterol	78 mg.
Fat	14 Gm.		

HUNGARIAN GOULASH

1 cup onion flakes
⅔ cup water
3 tablespoons vegetable oil
2½ lbs. lean boneless beef stew meat, cut in 1½-inch cubes
2 tablespoons paprika
1¾ teaspoons Morton Lite Salt mixture
¼ teaspoon pepper

¼ teaspoon powdered marjoram
2½ cups water
¾ cup dry white wine
¼ cup sweet pepper flakes
¼ cup flour
⅓ cup water

* * *

Poppyseed Noodles (page 171), (optional)

Mix onion flakes with ⅔ cup of water and let stand for 10 minutes. In a large Dutch oven or heavy skillet, heat 2 tablespoons of oil. Add onion; sauté for 5 minutes. Remove onion; set aside. Add remaining oil to pan. Add meat; brown well on all sides. Sprinkle with paprika, salt, pepper and marjoram. Stir in 2½ cups of water, wine, pepper flakes and sautéed onion. Bring to boil. Reduce heat; cover and simmer for 2 hours, or until meat is tender. Remove to serving platter. Strain gravy into saucepan. Mix flour with remaining ⅓ cup of water. Gradually blend into gravy. Cook, stirring constantly, until thickened. Spoon over beef cubes. If desired, serve with Poppyseed Noodles (page 171). Makes 8 servings.

Per Serving

Calories	258	Sodium	275 mg.
Carbohydrate	8 Gm.	Potassium	675 mg.
Protein	28 Gm.	Cholesterol	58 mg.
Fat	9 Gm.		

OLD-FASHIONED POT ROAST

1 lean brisket of beef (3½ lbs.)
2 tablespoons vegetable oil
1 cup cooked or canned tomatoes
1 cup water
1 teaspoon Morton Lite Salt mixture

1 small bay leaf
2 teaspoons onion powder
½ teaspoon coarse-ground black pepper
¼ teaspoon instant minced garlic

Brown meat in oil in large Dutch oven or heavy saucepan, turning so all sides are crusty. Add remaining ingredients. Cover* and simmer for 3 to 3¼ hours, or until tender, turning meat occasionally. Pour gravy into small bowl and place in freezer until fat forms hard layer across top. (Meantime, keep meat warm.) Discard fat layer. Return gravy to pan and heat until boiling. Makes 8 servings.

*Option: Bake, covered, at 325° for 3 to 3½ hours, or until tender.

Per Serving

Calories	196	Sodium	209 mg.
Carbohydrate	1 Gm.	Potassium	1050 mg.
Protein	24 Gm.	Cholesterol	70 mg.
Fat	10 Gm.		

ROAST VEAL

For a roast veal, buy leg, loin, rib (rack) or rolled shoulder. Place seasoned meat, fat side up, on a rack in an open pan. Bake at 300° to 325°. (A meat thermometer placed in the largest muscle will register 170° when veal is well done.) The following timetable will help.

Cut	Roasting Time
Leg, 5 to 8 lbs.	25–35 minutes per lb.
Loin, 4 to 6 lbs.	30–35 minutes per lb.
Rib (rack), 3 to 5 lbs.	35–40 minutes per lb.
Rolled shoulder, 4 to 6 lbs.	40–45 minutes per lb.

Per 4-oz. Serving

Calories	86	Sodium	62 mg.
Carbohydrate	0	Potassium	75 mg.
Protein	14 Gm.	Cholesterol	69 mg.
Fat	3 Gm.		

VEAL WITH LEMON

1½ lbs. veal round steak, boned
and cut ¼ inch thick
½ teaspoon Morton Lite Salt
mixture
Pepper
¼ cup flour
¼ cup vegetable oil
1 cup homemade chicken broth

½ teaspoon tarragon, crushed
1 teaspoon grated lemon peel
1 teaspoon fresh lemon juice
2 to 4 tablespoons water
* * *
Lemon Cartwheels
Minced parsley

Cut veal into serving pieces. Score edges to prevent curl-
ing. Season with salt and pepper and coat with flour.
Heat oil in large skillet. Add veal pieces, a few at a time,
and cook until browned on both sides. Remove from pan.
Drain off all but 1 tablespoon of pan drippings. Add
broth, tarragon, lemon peel and juice. Bring to a boil,
scraping drippings loose from bottom of pan. Add
browned cutlets; simmer very gently for 5 minutes or until
tender. Remove to warm serving platter. Add water to
drippings, using just enough to make sauce thin but not
watery. Add Lemon Cartwheels (see below) and heat just
a few seconds. Remove and top each serving with 1 or 2
Lemon Cartwheels; cover with sauce. Sprinkle generously
with snipped parsley and serve. Makes 6 servings.
Lemon Cartwheels: Use 1 large or 2 small lemons. Cut
away outer yellow peel, then peel again, leaving a thin but
intact layer of white membrane. (Without membrane, slices
will fall apart.) Slice lemons paper thin, less than ⅛ inch.
You will need 2 pretty slices for each piece of veal.

Per Serving

Calories	169	Sodium	261 mg.
Carbohydrate	4 Gm.	Potassium	417 mg.
Protein	15 Gm.	Cholesterol	72 mg.
Fat	10 Gm.		

ITALIAN VEAL CHOPS

½ cup vegetable oil
3 medium onions, sliced (4 cups)
6 veal chops, cut ½ inch thick
⅓ cup flour
½ cup water

2 tablespoons lemon juice
2 tablespoons chopped parsley
2 teaspoons Morton Lite Salt mixture
½ teaspoon oregano

Heat oil in large skillet over medium heat. Add onion; sauté about 5 minutes, or until slightly tender. Remove from skillet. Dredge veal chops with flour. Brown, turning once. Add onions with remaining ingredients. Cover and simmer for 25 to 30 minutes, or until meat is tender. Makes 6 servings.

Per Serving

Calories	365	Sodium	415 mg.
Carbohydrate	17 Gm.	Potassium	930 mg.
Protein	22 Gm.	Cholesterol	41 mg.
Fat	23 Gm.		

VEAL PAPRIKA

½ cup vegetable oil
3 medium onions, sliced (4 cups)
1 clove garlic, minced
2 lbs. veal shoulder, cut in 1-inch cubes
2 cups water
½ green pepper, cut in strips

3 tablespoons paprika
2 tablespoons chopped parsley
2 teaspoons Morton Lite Salt mixture
3 tablespoons cornstarch
* * *
Hot cooked noodles

Heat oil in large Dutch oven or kettle. Add onion and garlic; sauté until onion is tender. Remove. Add veal; brown on all sides, turning as needed. Add onion, 2 cups of water, green pepper, paprika, parsley and salt. Cover and simmer gently for 1 hour, or until tender. Mix together cornstarch and 2 tablespoons of water until smooth. Stir into veal mixture. Bring to boil, stirring constantly, and boil for 1 minute. Serve with hot noodles. Makes 6 servings.

Calories	314	Sodium	421 mg.
Carbohydrate	8 Gm.	Potassium	813 mg.
Protein	20 Gm.	Cholesterol	90 mg.
Fat	22 Gm.		

APPLE-STUFFED VEAL ROLLS

8 tablespoons (1 stick) unsalted polyunsaturated
margarine
½ cup chopped onion
3 cups day-old white bread
cubes
1 cup diced apple

½ teaspoon Morton Lite Salt
mixture
Generous dash pepper
1½ cups apple juice
1 lb. thin veal cutlets
        * * *
Chopped parsley

Melt 6 tablespoons of the margarine in a large skillet. Add
onion. Sauté, stirring occasionally, until golden, about 5
minutes. Stir in bread cubes. Heat, stirring, until margarine is absorbed. Stir in apple, salt, pepper and ¼ cup of
the apple juice; set aside. Place each veal cutlet between
sheets of waxed paper. Pound very thin with smooth-sur-
faced meat hammer or rolling pin; do not tear meat. Remove waxed paper. Top cutlets with apple mixture. Roll
up as for jelly roll. Fasten with toothpicks or tie with
string. Melt remaining 2 tablespoons of margarine in skillet. Add veal rolls. Brown on all sides over medium heat.
Add remaining 1¼ cups of apple juice and any remaining
stuffing. Cover; reduce heat and simmer for 30 to 35 minutes, or until veal is fork-tender and liquid is reduced to a
thick glaze. To serve, spoon glaze over veal, then sprinkle
with chopped parsley. Makes 4 servings.

Calories	568	Sodium	175 mg.
Carbohydrate	38 Gm.	Potassium	667 mg.
Protein	21 Gm.	Cholesterol	42 mg.
Fat	38 Gm.		

VEAL À LA MODE

1½ lbs. veal shoulder, cut in 2-inch cubes
1½ lbs. tomatoes, peeled and diced
1 small bay leaf
½ teaspoon powdered thyme
¼ teaspoon garlic powder
1 teaspoon Morton Lite Salt mixture
Dash pepper
4 small potatoes, peeled and cubed
1 package (10 oz.) frozen cut green beans

Spread veal cubes in a shallow baking pan. Brown on all sides under a hot broiler. Transfer meat with juices to a medium-size heavy saucepan. Add tomatoes and seasonings. Cover and simmer over low heat for 1 hour, or until meat is almost tender. Add potatoes and cook 15 minutes more. Add beans and continue cooking 15 minutes more. Makes 6 servings.

Per Serving

Calories	266	Sodium	220 mg.
Carbohydrate	19 Gm.	Potassium	827 mg.
Protein	21 Gm.	Cholesterol	42 mg.
Fat	12 Gm.		

ROAST LAMB

For roast lamb, buy a leg, a half leg, a rolled shoulder, a cushion shoulder or a rib cut. Season meat (use Morton Lite Salt mixture and pepper, and rub with a cut clove of garlic if desired) and place, fat side up, on a rack in an open pan. Bake at 300° to 325°. A meat thermometer inserted in the largest muscle will register 155° to 160° for rare, 165° to 170° for medium or 175° to 180° for well done. Use the following timetable as a rough guide:

	Approximate Cooking Time (Minutes per lb.)		
Cut	Rare	Medium	Well Done
Leg, 4 to 8 lbs.	25–27	28–30	32–34
Shoulder, 4 to 6 lbs.	25–27	28–30	30–35
Rolled, 3 to 5 lbs.	25–27	28–30	35–45
Cushion, 3 to 5 lbs.	25–27	28–30	30–35
Rib, 1½ to 3 lbs.*	25–27	28–31	35–45

*Roast rib at 375°.

Calories	96	Sodium	41 mg.
Carbohydrate	0	Potassium	210 mg.
Protein	14 Gm.	Cholesterol	49 mg.
Fat	4 Gm.		

BROILED LAMB

The cuts of lamb that can be broiled are shoulder chops, rib chops, loin chops and ground lamb patties. Grease the broiling rack before placing lamb on it. Preheat the broiler if needed. If lamb is ¾ to 1 inch thick, set rack so top surface of meat is 2 to 3 inches from source of heat. Place it 3 to 5 inches away if cut is 1 to 2 inches thick. Broil until top side is brown, season with Morton Lite Salt mixture and pepper, then turn and brown other side. Season again and serve. Use the timetable below as a rough guide:

Cut	Total Approximate Cooking Time, Minutes		
	Thickness	*Rare*	*Medium*
Shoulder chops	1 inch	6–7	12
	1½ inches	9–10	18
Rib chops	1 inch	6–7	12
	1½ inches	9–10	18
	2 inches	12–14	22
Loin chops	1 inch	6–7	12
	1½ inches	8–9	18
	2 inches	9–10	22
Ground lamb patties	1 inch	10–12	18

Broiled 1½-inch rib chop

Calories	119	Sodium	54 mg.
Carbohydrate	0	Potassium	384 mg.
Protein	10 Gm.	Cholesterol	57 mg.
Fat	8 Gm.		

LAMB, GREEK STYLE

1 5-lb. leg of lamb
1 tablespoon Morton Lite
  Salt mixture
2 teaspoons crushed oregano
¼ teaspoon pepper

½ cup flour
2 cloves garlic, crushed
1 teaspoon grated lemon peel
⅓ cup lemon juice
¼ to ⅓ cup water

With point of sharp knife, make slashes about 2 inches apart over entire surface of roast, cutting about ½ inch deep and ¾ inch long. Thoroughly combine seasonings, flour, garlic and lemon peel. Add only enough lemon juice to form a smooth not too thick paste. Rub over entire roast, working it into each opening with fingers.

Place on rack in shallow roasting pan. Bake at 350° for 1¾ hours. If meat thermometer is available, insert it now and continue baking until dial registers 180°, for 40 to 45 minutes more. Carefully lift out lamb to carving board or platter and let stand for 10 to 15 minutes. Meanwhile transfer drippings into small saucepan; skim off fat. Blend in water; heat and serve with lamb. Makes 8 servings.

Per Serving

Calories	269	Sodium	515 mg.
Carbohydrate	6 Gm.	Potassium	925 mg.
Protein	35 Gm.	Cholesterol	122 mg.
Fat	10 Gm.		

SHISH KABOB

Marinade:

⅔ cup vegetable oil
⅓ cup wine vinegar
1 tablespoon Morton Lite Salt
  mixture
½ teaspoon crushed rosemary

¼ teaspoon coarse-ground
  black pepper
1 bay leaf
1 clove garlic, minced

Kabobs:

1 lb. boneless lamb, cut in 1½-
  inch cubes
6 to 8 small white onions, parboiled

½ lb. large mushroom caps
1 tomato, cut in wedges
1 medium green pepper, cut in
  2-inch pieces

Combine ingredients for marinade in shallow dish. Prick lamb cubes; add, with vegetables, to marinade. Cover and refrigerate for at least 3 hours, or overnight, turning frequently. Arrange marinated meat and vegetables separately on metal skewers. (Vegetables will cook more quickly than the meat.) Broil 3 inches from heat, turning occasionally, about 15 minutes or until tender. Makes 4 servings.

Per Serving

Calories	244	Sodium	324 mg.
Carbohydrate	5 Gm.	Potassium	816 mg.
Protein	15 Gm.	Cholesterol	49 mg.
Fat	18 Gm.		

ARMENIAN GROUND LAMB KABOBS

½ cup instant minced onion
¾ cup water
2 tablespoons unsalted polyunsaturated margarine
2 lbs. lean ground lamb
1 lightly beaten egg

2 tablespoons parsley flakes
1¾ teaspoons Morton Lite Salt mixture
¾ teaspoon ground cumin
⅛ teaspoon coarse-ground black pepper
12 cherry tomatoes

Mix onion and water and let stand for 10 minutes. In small skillet, melt margarine. Add half the onion and cook gently for 4 minutes. In a large mixing bowl, combine the sautéed onion with lamb, egg, parsley flakes, salt, cumin and black pepper. Mix well. Shape into small oblongs about 2 inches long and ¾ inch in diameter. Arrange meat and tomatoes on separate skewers. (Tomatoes will cook more quickly than meat.) Broil 3 inches from heat for 10 to 12 minutes, or until done to taste, turning often. Makes 6 servings.

Per Serving

Calories	192	Sodium	390 mg.
Carbohydrate	3 Gm.	Potassium	718 mg.
Protein	20 Gm.	Cholesterol	111 mg.
Fat	10 Gm.		

LAMB STEW

⅓ cup flour
1½ teaspoons Morton Lite
Salt mixture
⅛ teaspoon pepper
1½ lbs. boneless stew lamb,
cut in 1-inch cubes
2 tablespoons oil

3¼ cups water
3 medium onions, sliced
4 medium potatoes, cut into
1-inch cubes
5 medium carrots, quartered
1½ cups fresh peas

Combine flour, salt and pepper; coat lamb cubes thoroughly with mixture. Heat oil in Dutch oven or deep kettle. Add lamb and brown on all sides. Empty remaining seasoned flour out of bag over lamb; stir. Add water; cover tightly. Simmer 1½ to 2 hours, or until lamb is tender. Add onions, potatoes and carrots; simmer, covered, for 15 minutes. Add peas. Simmer, covered, until vegetables are all tender, stirring occasionally. Makes 6 servings.

Per Serving

Calories	258	Sodium	322 mg.
Carbohydrate	25 Gm.	Potassium	925 mg.
Protein	18 Gm.	Cholesterol	49 mg.
Fat	9 Gm.		

LAMB CURRY

3 tablespoons flour
1 teaspoon Morton Lite Salt
mixture
1½ lbs. boneless stew lamb,
cut in 1-inch cubes
2 tablespoons unsalted polyunsaturated margarine
1 medium-size onion, sliced

1 medium-size tart apple,
diced
1 tablespoon curry powder
¾ cup orange juice
* * *
Rice (optional)
Garnish: Pineapple cubes,
chopped peanuts or pecans
(optional)

Blend flour and salt; coat lamb cubes thoroughly with mixture. Heat margarine in skillet. Add lamb and brown on all sides. Add onion, apple and curry powder; cook for 2 to 4 minutes, or until onion is tender. Add orange juice and simmer, covered, until lamb is tender, about 1 hour.

Check liquid occasionally. If mixture seems dry, add a bit of water. Good with rice; may be garnished with heated canned pineapple cubes and chopped peanuts or pecans. Makes 4 servings.

Per Serving

Calories	274	Sodium	341 mg.
Carbohydrate	17 Gm.	Potassium	844 mg.
Protein	22 Gm.	Cholesterol	73 mg.
Fat	13 Gm.		

ROAST PORK

All the cuts in the chart below may be roasted. Preheat the oven to 325°. Place the roast on a rack, fat side up. Season with Morton Lite Salt mixture and pepper and, if desired, rub with grated lemon peel. A meat thermometer in the largest muscle will register 170° when pork is well done. Use the timetable below to help in planning:

Cut		Weight	Cooking Time (Minutes per lb.)
Loin	Center	3–5 lbs.	30–35
	Half	5–7 lbs.	35–40
	Rolled	3–5 lbs.	35–45
Picnic shoulder		5–8 lbs.	30–35
	Rolled	3–5 lbs.	35–40
Fresh ham, whole, bone in		12–16 lbs.	22–26
whole, rolled		10–14 lbs.	24–28
half, bone in		5–8 lbs.	35–40

Per 4-oz. Serving

Calories	116	Sodium	34 mg.
Carbohydrate	0	Potassium	190 mg.
Protein	12 Gm.	Cholesterol	44 mg.
Fat	7 Gm.		

BROILED PORK CHOPS

Have rib or loin pork chops cut ¾ to 1 inch thick. Place on rack of broiling pan. Preheat broiler if needed. Place pan in broiler so top of meat is 2 to 3 inches from source of heat. Broil until top side is brown, about 12 minutes. Season with Morton Lite Salt mixture and pepper. Turn and cook for 8 to 12 minutes more.

Per Broiled Pork Chop (¾ inch)

Calories	314	Sodium	184 mg.
Carbohydrate	0	Potassium	500 mg.
Protein	26 Gm.	Cholesterol	76 mg.
Fat	23 Gm.		

APPLE-STUFFED PORK CHOPS

¼ cup instant minced onion	1½ teaspoons Morton Lite Salt mixture
½ cup water	⅛ teaspoon ground pepper
1 tablespoon unsalted polyunsaturated margarine	1 lightly beaten egg
1¾ cups toasted small bread cubes	6 rib pork chops, 1 inch thick, with pocket
½ cup diced peeled apple	1 tablespoon vegetable oil
¾ teaspoon poultry seasoning	1½ cups orange juice

Mix onion with ¼ cup of the water; let stand 10 minutes. In a small skillet, melt margarine, add onion, and cook gently for 5 minutes. In a mixing bowl, blend onion with bread cubes, apple, poultry seasoning, ½ teaspoon of the salt, pepper, egg and the remaining ¼ cup of water. Spoon about 2 tablespoons of this stuffing into the pocket of each pork chop. Fasten with toothpicks. Sprinkle with remaining salt and add pepper to taste. Heat the oil in a heavy skillet. Add pork chops and brown on both sides. If skillet is ovenproof, use as casserole; otherwise, transfer chops into shallow baking dish. Pour orange juice over all. Cover and bake at 375° for 1 hour, or until tender. Makes 6 servings.

Calories	641	Sodium	343 mg.
Carbohydrate	16 Gm.	Potassium	1075 mg.
Protein	30 Gm.	Cholesterol	153 mg.
Fat	50 Gm.		

PORK CHOPS JARDINIÈRE

1 tablespoon vegetable oil
4 loin pork chops
½ cup chopped onion
1 tablespoon flour
1 cup chopped, peeled tomatoes
½ cup orange juice

½ cup water
1½ teaspoons Morton Lite Salt mixture
½ teaspoon crushed thyme
1 avocado, peeled and sliced
2 oranges, peeled and sliced

Heat oil in skillet. Add pork chops and brown on both sides. Remove. Add onion to skillet and cook until tender. Sprinkle with flour; stir to mix well. Add tomatoes, orange juice, water, salt and thyme. Add pork chops, turn to coat. Cover and simmer for 1 hour, or until meat is tender, turning once. Add sliced avocado and oranges; heat through. Makes 4 servings.

Per Serving

Calories	507	Sodium	472 mg.
Carbohydrate	22 Gm.	Potassium	1300 mg.
Protein	29 Gm.	Cholesterol	76 mg.
Fat	35 Gm.		

OLD-FASHIONED STUFFED CABBAGE

1 head (3 lbs.) green cabbage
1 lb. ground lean pork
½ lb. ground lean beef
1½ cups cooked rice
2 tablespoons parsley flakes
1½ teaspoons Morton Lite
Salt mixture
1 teaspoon onion powder
¼ teaspoon ground red pepper
1 can (1 lb.) tomatoes, broken up
1 can (8 oz.) tomato sauce
1 teaspoon dill seed
½ teaspoon sugar
Dash pepper

Core the cabbage. Place it in a large kettle containing boiling water to cover. Cook until leaves separate from head, removing them as this occurs. Drain leaves. Trim thick center vein from cabbage leaves, being careful not to tear leaves. Set leaves aside.

In a mixing bowl, combine pork, beef, rice, parsley flakes, 1¼ teaspoons of salt, onion powder and red pepper. Mix well. Place a heaping tablespoon of filling in the center of each leaf. Fold 2 sides over filling; roll up. In a Dutch oven or large skillet, place leftover cabbage. Lay stuffed cabbage on top, seam side up. Combine tomatoes, tomato sauce, dill seed, sugar, ¼ teaspoon salt and pepper; mix well. Pour over stuffed cabbage. Cover; bring to boiling point. Reduce heat and simmer 2 to 2½ hours. Makes 10 portions, or 26 cabbage rolls.

Per Serving

Calories	177	Sodium	361 mg.
Carbohydrate	18 Gm.	Potassium	62 mg.
Protein	13 Gm.	Cholesterol	30 mg.
Fat	6 Gm.		

ENROLLADOS

6 medium tomatoes (2 lbs.), diced
2 cups shredded cooked pork*
½ cup chopped onion
1 clove garlic, minced
1½ cups diced cooked potatoes
2 tablespoons unsalted polyunsaturated margarine

1¾ teaspoons Morton Lite Salt mixture
½ teaspoon pepper
½ teaspoon crushed red pepper
12 tortillas
1 small head lettuce, shredded
½ cup fresh onion rings
1 tablespoon vegetable oil
¼ teaspoon ground oregano

Purée tomatoes in blender. Strain and set aside. In large skillet, cook pork, onion, garlic, potatoes and ⅓ of the puréed tomatoes in margarine for 10 minutes. Add 1¼ teaspoons of salt, ¼ teaspoon of pepper and red pepper. Heat tortillas as directed on package. Spoon 2 tablespoons of this mixture on each. Roll up and arrange on shredded lettuce. Sauté onion rings in oil in skillet. Add remaining tomato purée, salt, pepper and oregano. Mix well. Cook for 5 minutes. Spoon over Enrollados. Makes 6 servings.

*Option: Shredded chicken or turkey may be substituted.

Per Serving

Calories	252	Sodium	334 mg.
Carbohydrate	42 Gm.	Potassium	1016 mg.
Protein	6 Gm.	Cholesterol	88 mg.
Fat	8 Gm.		

Poultry

Most of us are eating more poultry today than we did twenty years ago. Both chicken and turkey are relatively inexpensive forms of protein. They, and their somewhat more expensive cousin, the rock Cornish hen, are also fairly low in saturated fat.

Following are some recipes, both basics and more complex ones, to keep your family happily eating poultry once or twice a week. A word of caution: Duck and goose are higher in fat and should be avoided from a calorie standpoint.

ROAST CHICKEN

Buy whole chickens as large as possible. Wash inside and out with cold water, drain, then sprinkle neck and body cavities with 1 teaspoon of Morton Lite Salt mixture per chicken. If desired, stuff. Hook wing tip onto back to hold neck skin; tie legs together, then to tail. Place chicken directly in shallow pan; a rack is unnecessary. If desired, brush chicken with vegetable oil. Roast according to timetable. If chicken is stuffed, increase total roasting time by 15 minutes. To test for doneness, drumstick meat should feel soft when pressed between fingers and leg should twist easily out of thigh joint. If bird is 2 pounds or less, roast at 400°. Chickens over 2 pounds should be roasted at 375°.

Weight	Time (per lb.)	Approx. Amount Stuffing	Approx. Total Time
1½ lbs.	40 min.	¾ cup	1 hr.
2 lbs.	35 min.	1 cup	1 hr. 10 min.
2½ lbs.	30 min.	1¼ cups	1 hr. 15 min.
3 lbs.	30 min.	1½ cups	1 hr. 30 min.
3½ lbs.	30 min.	1¾ cups	1 hr. 45 min.
4 lbs.	30 min.	2 cups	2 hrs.
4½ lbs.	30 min.	2¼ cups	2 hrs. 15 min.
5 lbs.	30 min.	2½ cups	2 hrs. 30 min.

Per 6-oz. Serving

Calories	256	Sodium	642 mg.
Carbohydrate	26 Gm.	Potassium	662 mg.
Protein	22 Gm.	Cholesterol	67 mg.
Fat	7 Gm.		

RICE STUFFING FOR CHICKEN

¾ cup uncooked long-grain rice
⅓ cup unsalted polyunsaturated margarine
½ cup chopped onion

½ cup chopped green pepper
½ teaspoon sage
¼ teaspoon thyme
⅛ teaspoon pepper

Cook rice according to package directions, using Morton Lite Salt mixture. Melt margarine in skillet. Add chopped onion and green pepper; cook, stirring occasionally, until tender. Add cooked rice, sage, thyme and pepper. Toss lightly with fork. Use to stuff chicken. Enough for one 4-pound bird. Serves 5.

Per Recipe

Calories	209	Sodium	8 mg.
Carbohydrate	18 Gm.	Potassium	68 mg.
Protein	2 Gm.	Cholesterol	0
Fat	15 Gm.		

FOIL-ROASTED CHICKEN WITH VEGETABLES

1 whole broiler-fryer chicken (2½ to 3 lbs.)
Morton Lite Salt mixture
Pepper
Paprika
4 carrots, pared and sliced

1 lb. green beans, cut into pieces, or 1 package (10 oz.) frozen cut green beans
2 large potatoes, peeled and cut into quarters

* * *

Chopped parsley

Sprinkle chicken cavity with salt and pepper. Hook wing tip onto back to hold neck skin; tie legs together. Place chicken across center of a 24-inch piece of heavy-duty aluminum foil. Sprinkle with paprika. Arrange vegetables around chicken. Sprinkle with more salt and pepper. Bring ends of foil together over chicken; make a double fold and another double fold at each end. Place in a shallow roasting pan. Bake at 450° for 1 hour. Open foil and fold back; roast for 20 minutes longer. Sprinkle with chopped parsley and remove to serving platter. Serves 4.

Per Serving

Calories	314	Sodium	267 mg.
Carbohydrate	14 Gm.	Potassium	1400 mg.
Protein	37 Gm.	Cholesterol	109 mg.
Fat	11 Gm.		

LEMON-BROILED CHICKEN

¼ cup lemon juice
1 teaspoon grated lemon peel
1 teaspoon vegetable oil
½ teaspoon Morton Lite Salt mixture
½ teaspoon ground ginger
½ teaspoon paprika
¼ teaspoon onion powder
¼ teaspoon pepper
1 broiler-fryer chicken, 2½ lbs., quartered

In a small bowl, combine all ingredients except chicken; mix well. Brush over chicken. Place on broiling pan, skin side down. Broil 9 inches from heat source for 20 minutes. Turn. Continue broiling, turning and basting occasionally until browned and crisp, for 25 minutes, or until done. Makes 4 servings.

Per Serving

Calories	233	Sodium	189 mg.
Protein	2 Gm.	Potassium	1000 mg.
Carbohydrate	30 Gm.	Cholesterol	91 mg.
Fat	11 Gm.		

SIMMERED CHICKEN

1 broiler-fryer chicken, whole or cut in serving pieces
2 cups water
1 small onion, sliced
3 celery tops
1 teaspoon Morton Lite Salt mixture
¼ teaspoon pepper

Put chicken in a large pot; add water and remaining ingredients. Bring to a boil; cover tightly. Reduce heat and simmer for 1 hour, or until tender, adding extra water as needed. Remove from heat; strain broth and, if desired, store in a covered jar in the refrigerator. When chicken is cool, remove meat from skin and cut into chunks for use in salads or other dishes. One broiler-fryer yields about 2½ cups of cut-up cooked chicken and 2 to 2½ cups broth. Serves 5.

Per Serving

Calories	215	Sodium	225 mg.
Carbohydrate	2 Gm.	Potassium	736 mg.
Protein	27 Gm.	Cholesterol	80 mg.
Fat	10 Gm.		

PEAR CHICKEN BAKE

1 can (1 lb. 13 oz.) Bartlett pear halves
1 can (8 oz.) crushed pineapple
1 can (6 oz.) frozen pineapple-grapefruit concentrate
1 teaspoon Morton Lite Salt mixture
¼ teaspoon curry powder
¼ teaspoon ginger
½ cup unsalted polyunsaturated margarine
1 broiler-fryer chicken, 3 to 4 lbs., cut up
2 teaspoons cornstarch

Drain pears, reserving syrup. Drain pineapple and measure ½ cup of fruit. Set aside. Pour remaining pineapple and pineapple syrup into saucepan. Add juice concentrate, ½ cup of pear syrup, seasonings and margarine. Heat to boiling. Place chicken parts in shallow baking pan and baste with hot fruit mixture. Bake at 375° for 1 hour, or until tender, basting frequently. Fill pear halves with reserved pineapple; brush with basting sauce and broil until lightly browned, or bake at 375° for 10 minutes. Pour basting sauce into saucepan. Add a little to cornstarch and return to remaining basting sauce. Cook, stirring constantly, until thickened. Serve hot pear halves and sauce with chicken. Makes 6 servings.

Per Serving

Calories	398	Sodium	228 mg.
Carbohydrate	21 Gm.	Potassium	869 mg.
Protein	24 Gm.	Cholesterol	72 mg.
Fat	23 Gm.		

HERB-BAKED CHICKEN WITH WINE SAUCE

¼ cup unsalted polyunsaturated margarine, softened
1 teaspoon Morton Lite Salt mixture
⅛ teaspoon pepper
⅛ teaspoon rosemary
⅛ teaspoon thyme

Generous dash garlic powder
Generous dash onion powder
4 chicken breasts (about 1½ lbs.)
1 cup water
2 tablespoons flour
2 tablespoons dry white wine

Combine margarine and seasonings. Arrange chicken breasts, skin side down, in large baking dish. Spread half the margarine mixture on chicken. Bake at 400° for 30 minutes. Turn chicken; spread with remaining margarine mixture. Bake for 30 minutes longer, or until done. Remove chicken to serving platter; keep warm. Gradually blend water into flour. Stir into drippings. Heat, stirring, until thickened. Add wine; heat. Serve sauce over chicken. Makes 4 servings.

Per Serving

Calories	248	Sodium	368 mg.
Carbohydrate	4 Gm.	Potassium	150 mg.
Protein	24 Gm.	Cholesterol	81 mg.
Fat	13 Gm.		

OVEN-FRIED CHICKEN

1 broiler-fryer chicken, 2½ to 3 lbs., cut up
½ cup fine dry bread crumbs or flour

2 teaspoons Morton Lite Salt mixture
1 teaspoon paprika
¼ teaspoon pepper
¼ cup vegetable oil

Wash chicken and pat dry. Mix together bread crumbs or flour with salt, paprika and pepper. Coat chicken with this mixture. Pour oil in shallow baking pan. Arrange chicken pieces in pan, skin side down. Bake at 400° for 30 minutes. Turn chicken and continue baking about 30 minutes, or until tender. Makes 4 servings.

Calories	417	Sodium	691 mg.
Carbohydrate	8 Gm.	Potassium	1433 mg.
Protein	37 Gm.	Cholesterol	113 mg.
Fat	25 Gm.		

CHICKEN WITH PEACHES

1 broiler-fryer, 2½ to 3½ lbs., cut up and skinned
½ teaspoon Morton Lite Salt mixture
½ cup flour

1 can (1 lb. 13 oz.) peach halves or slices
¼ cup unsalted polyunsaturated margarine
⅓ cup orange juice
½ cup walnuts

Wash chicken and pat dry. Sprinkle with salt and coat with flour, shaking off excess. Place in medium shallow baking dish. Drain peaches, saving ¾ cup of syrup. Melt margarine in small saucepan; stir in orange juice and peach syrup. Pour over chicken. Bake at 375°, basting several times with juices in dish, for 1 hour. Add peaches and walnuts and continue baking, basting once, for 15 minutes, or until chicken is tender and glazed. Makes 4 servings.

Per Serving

Calories	575	Sodium	202 mg.
Carbohydrate	35 Gm.	Potassium	1100 mg.
Protein	39 Gm.	Cholesterol	109 mg.
Fat	31 Gm.		

BAKED CHICKEN WITH GRAPES

1 broiler-fryer chicken, about 2½ lbs., cut up
1 cup water
2 tablespoons finely chopped onion
1 teaspoon Morton Lite Salt mixture
¾ teaspoon thyme
¼ teaspoon pepper
⅛ teaspoon minced garlic
4 teaspoons cornstarch
4 teaspoons water
1 cup seedless green grapes
1 tablespoon cooking sherry

Wash chicken and pat dry. Place in shallow baking dish, about 15″ × 10″. Add water. Combine onion, salt, thyme, pepper and garlic; sprinkle over chicken. Bake, uncovered, at 350° for 1½ hours, or until tender. Remove chicken to serving dish. Drain drippings into saucepan. Add cornstarch mixed with water and stir over medium heat until thickened. Add grapes and sherry and heat through. Pass this sauce with the chicken. Makes 4 servings.

Per Serving

Calories	234	Sodium	328 mg.
Carbohydrate	4 Gm.	Potassium	1031 mg.
Protein	30 Gm.	Cholesterol	91 mg.
Fat	9 Gm.		

CHICKEN CACCIATORE

1 broiler-fryer, 2½ to 3½ lbs., cut up
¼ cup flour
¼ cup vegetable oil
1 medium onion, chopped
1 medium green pepper, chopped
1 clove garlic, minced
1¼ teaspoons Morton Lite Salt mixture
⅛ teaspoon pepper
2 bay leaves
1 can (1 lb.) whole tomatoes, cut up
1 can (8 oz.) tomato sauce

* * *

2 tablespoons chopped parsley

Wash chicken and pat dry. Coat with flour. Heat oil in large skillet. Add chicken and cook over medium heat, turning as needed, until lightly browned on all sides. Remove from skillet. Add onion, green pepper and garlic to oil and cook about 3 minutes. Add chicken; spoon sautéed vegetables over chicken. Add salt, pepper, bay

76

leaves, tomatoes and tomato sauce. Cover and simmer for 25 minutes, or until chicken is tender. Remove bay leaves. Serve garnished with parsley. Makes 4 servings.

Per Serving

Calories	514	Sodium	608 mg.
Carbohydrate	19 Gm.	Potassium	1287 mg.
Protein	40 Gm.	Cholesterol	109 mg.
Fat	31 Gm.		

CHICKEN SCALLOPINE

8 chicken thighs, boned*	2 tablespoons chopped parsley
1 teaspoon Morton Lite Salt mixture	1 tablespoon chopped chives
	¼ teaspoon marjoram
2 tablespoons unsalted polyunsaturated margarine	* * *
	Buttered toast points or rice
1 tablespoon lemon juice	Lemon slices (optional)

Place boned thighs between two pieces of waxed paper. Pound with side of cleaver or rolling pin to flatten. Sprinkle with salt. Melt margarine over medium heat in large skillet. Add chicken, skin side down. Cook about 10 minutes, or until lightly browned. Turn; sprinkle with lemon juice and herbs. Cook about 10 minutes more, until tender. Serve on buttered toast points or rice. If desired, garnish with thin lemon slices. Makes 4 servings.

*To bone chicken thighs: Make a lengthwise cut along thinner side of a broiler-fryer thigh. Scrape flesh away from bone and remove bone.

Per Serving

Calories	185	Sodium	363 mg.
Carbohydrate	4 Gm.	Potassium	1005 mg.
Protein	21 Gm.	Cholesterol	78 mg.
Fat	17 Gm.		

CHICKEN PICCATA

1½ lbs. boned, skinned chicken breasts (3 breasts)
¼ cup unsalted polyunsaturated margarine
1 tablespoon flour
1 teaspoon Morton Lite Salt mixture
1 teaspoon tarragon

½ cup homemade chicken broth
3 thin lemon slices, halved

* * *

Rice (optional)
1 teaspoon finely chopped parsley

Cut chicken breasts into narrow strips. Have all other ingredients ready, and make this dish when the remaining parts of the meal are nearly done. Melt margarine in a large skillet over high heat. Add chicken; sprinkle with flour, salt and tarragon. Cook for 5 minutes, stirring constantly. Add chicken broth and lemon slices; stir to loosen any browned particles. Cover and cook for 2 to 3 minutes. Serve over rice, if desired, or as an appetizer. Sprinkle with chopped parsley. Makes 3 servings.

Per Serving

Calories	278	Sodium	122 mg.
Carbohydrate	2 Gm.	Potassium	700 mg.
Protein	24 Gm.	Cholesterol	87 mg.
Fat	18 Gm.		

POLYNESIAN CHICKEN

2 broiler-fryer chickens, 2½ to 3 lbs. each, cut up
2 teaspoons Morton Lite Salt mixture
1 tablespoon paprika
¼ teaspoon pepper
Vegetable oil
1 can (13½ oz.) pineapple chunks
½ cup orange juice

2 tablespoons lemon juice
¼ cup dark corn syrup
¼ teaspoon mace
⅛ teaspoon ground ginger
1 tablespoon flour
2 tablespoons water
2 oranges, peeled and sliced

* * *

Rice (optional)

Sprinkle chicken with mixture of salt, paprika and pepper. Heat oil in large skillet; brown chicken on all sides. Drain off excess fat. Drain pineapple, saving ½ cup of syrup.

Combine this syrup with orange and lemon juice, corn syrup, mace and ginger. Pour over chicken in skillet. Cover and simmer for 30 minutes, or until tender. Remove chicken to warm serving platter. Mix flour and water together until smooth; slowly stir into sauce in pan; boil for 2 to 3 minutes. Add drained pineapple and orange slices; heat just until warm. Pour over chicken and serve at once. Serve with rice if desired. Makes 8 servings.

Per Serving

Calories	360	Sodium	337 mg.
Carbohydrate	16 Gm.	Potassium	841 mg.
Protein	36 Gm.	Cholesterol	109 mg.
Fat	16 Gm.		

CRANBERRY-ALMOND CHICKEN

1 broiler-fryer chicken, about 3 lbs., cut up
1 teaspoon Morton Lite Salt mixture
¼ teaspoon pepper
1 teaspoon paprika
⅓ cup unsalted polyunsaturated margarine
1 cup cranberry juice cocktail
½ cup slivered almonds, toasted

Wash chicken and pat dry. Combine salt, pepper and paprika; rub into chicken. Melt margarine in large skillet. Add chicken and brown on all sides. Cover frying pan, reduce heat, and cook for 25 to 30 minutes, or until chicken is tender. Remove to warm platter and keep hot in warm oven. Pour cranberry cocktail into frying pan; stir to loosen all browned particles. Cook over high heat until only ½ cup remains. Pour over chicken. Sprinkle with toasted almonds and serve at once. Makes 4 servings.

Per Serving

Calories	532	Sodium	338 mg.
Carbohydrate	15 Gm.	Potassium	1147 mg.
Protein	40 Gm.	Cholesterol	108 mg.
Fat	36 Gm.		

MOO GOO GAI PAN

1 lb. boned and skinned chicken breasts (2 breasts)
½ teaspoon Morton Lite Salt mixture
⅛ teaspoon pepper
2 tablespoons vegetable oil
2 tablespoons sliced green onions
1 cup sliced fresh mushrooms
2 tablespoons sliced pimiento

¼ teaspoon ground ginger
1 cup homemade chicken broth
1 package (about 7 oz.) frozen snow peas, thawed enough to separate
1 tablespoon cornstarch
2 tablespoons water

* * *

Hot cooked rice

Cut chicken into 1-inch cubes. Sprinkle with salt and pepper. Heat oil in skillet over medium heat. Add chicken; cook, stirring constantly, until chicken turns white throughout. Remove from skillet. Add green onions and cook 1 minute; stir in mushrooms, pimiento and ginger; cook for 3 to 5 minutes, or until mushrooms are tender. Add broth and snow peas. Bring to boil, separating snow peas with fork. Mix cornstarch and water until smooth; stir into vegetable mixture. Bring to boil, stirring constantly, and boil for 1 minute. Return chicken to skillet. Reduce heat to low; cook for 2 to 3 minutes, or until chicken is hot. Serve with rice. Makes 4 servings.

Per Serving

Calories	177	Sodium	232 mg.
Carbohydrate	11 Gm.	Potassium	522 mg.
Protein	15 Gm.	Cholesterol	39 mg.
Fat	8 Gm.		

JELLIED ORANGE CHICKEN SALAD

2 envelopes unflavored gelatin
¼ cup sugar
¼ teaspoon Morton Lite Salt mixture
2 cups water
1 can (6 oz.) frozen orange juice concentrate, undiluted
½ cup tarragon vinegar

4 oranges, peeled and sectioned
1 cup diced cooked chicken or 1 can (6 oz.) chicken, diced
½ cup minced celery

* * *

Lettuce leaves

Mix gelatin, sugar and salt in saucepan. Stir in 1 cup of the water. Place over low heat, stirring constantly, until gelatin and sugar are dissolved (about 3 to 5 minutes). Stir in remaining cup of water, undiluted orange concentrate and tarragon vinegar. Mix well. Chill until mixture is slightly thicker than unbeaten egg whites. Meanwhile, cut enough orange sections in half to make ½ cup; fold into gelatin mixture with chicken and celery. Turn into 1½-quart mold. Chill until firm. Unmold; garnish with greens and remaining orange sections. If desired, serve with mayonnaise thinned with orange juice. Makes 6 servings.

Per Serving

Calories	219	Sodium	47 mg.
Carbohydrate	35 Gm.	Potassium	577 mg.
Protein	14 Gm.	Cholesterol	20 mg.
Fat	4 Gm.		

CHICKEN SALAD WITH RICE AND AVOCADOS

4 teaspoons lemon juice
1½ cups diced avocado
1 cup cooked, diced chicken
1½ cups cooked rice
½ cup finely chopped celery
1 tablespoon finely chopped green onion

2 tablespoons mayonnaise
2 tablespoons sour cream
1 teaspoon Morton Lite Salt mixture

* * *

Lettuce leaves

Toss lemon juice lightly with avocado. Combine remaining ingredients, except lettuce, and mix well. Add avocado and toss lightly. Chill thoroughly. Serve on crisp lettuce, as a side dish at buffets or a light luncheon dish with finger sandwiches. Makes 4 servings.

Per Serving

Calories	316	Sodium	562 mg.
Carbohydrate	18 Gm.	Potassium	834 mg.
Protein	17 Gm.	Cholesterol	53 mg.
Fat	19 Gm.		

HERBED CHICKEN LIVERS

1 lb. chicken livers, cut in half
¾ teaspoon Morton Lite Salt mixture
⅛ teaspoon pepper
1 tablespoon chopped onion

1 tablespoon chopped parsley
½ teaspoon tarragon
Flour
2 tablespoons unsalted polyunsaturated margarine

Sprinkle livers with salt, pepper, onion, parsley and tarragon. Dust lightly with a little flour. Melt margarine in skillet over medium heat. Add livers and cook about 10 minutes, turning occasionally. Makes 4 servings.

Option: If desired, add ½ cup of dry white wine to pan drippings. Increase heat and cook, stirring constantly, until slightly thickened. Pour over chicken livers.

Per Serving

Calories	222	Sodium	207 mg.
Carbohydrate	5 Gm.	Potassium	450 mg.
Protein	25 Gm.	Cholesterol	340 mg.
Fat	11 Gm.		

TURKEY

Since most turkey is available frozen, buy a reputable brand and follow the label directions for thawing and roasting. To stuff the turkey you may use a packaged stuffing mix, following package directions, or try the recipe below:

SESAME SEED STUFFING

½ cup celery flakes
¼ cup instant minced onion
⅔ cup water
1 cup unsalted polyunsaturated margarine
3 quarts toasted bread cubes
1 cup toasted sesame seeds*

⅓ cup parsley flakes
1 tablespoon Morton Lite Salt mixture
¾ teaspoon pepper
¾ cup homemade chicken or turkey broth

Mix celery flakes and onion with water and let stand for 10 minutes. Melt margarine in medium skillet. Add celery and onion and cook until golden. In a large bowl, combine remaining ingredients. Add sautéed celery and onion. Use to stuff neck and body cavity of 12- to 15-pound turkey.

To toast sesame seeds: Sprinkle in a large shallow pan. Toast at 350° for 8 to 10 minutes, or until golden.

Per Serving

Calories	452	Sodium	369 mg.
Carbohydrate	31 Gm.	Potassium	480 mg.
Protein	91 Gm.	Cholesterol	12 mg.
Fat	34 Gm.		

COUNTRY GARDEN CORNISH HENS

2 Rock Cornish game hens, 17 to 22 oz. each, dressed and frozen
⅔ cup sliced celery
⅔ cup sliced onion
½ cup sliced carrots
¼ cup vegetable oil
2 teaspoons Morton Lite Salt mixture
¼ to ½ teaspoon pepper
⅓ cup melted unsalted polyunsaturated margarine
⅓ cup sherry

Thaw hens for 2 to 4 hours at room temperature, or for a day in the refrigerator. Remove giblets and save for another use. With kitchen shears or sharp heavy knife, cut hens in half along breastbone and backbone. Wipe pieces with damp paper towel. Grease a shallow casserole or 9-inch baking pan. Mix vegetables. Arrange in pan in four mounds. Brush or rub hen halves with oil, using 1 tablespoon per half hen. Sprinkle each hen half with salt, using ½ teaspoon for each; then sprinkle each with pepper. With cavity side down, put a hen half on each mound of vegetables. Roast at 375° for about 1 hour, or until juice from hens is no longer pink and the meat is tender. Brush or drizzle melted margarine over hens, using a generous tablespoon for each half. Add sherry to pan. Return to oven for 5 to 10 minutes longer. Or broil for 3 minutes, until golden. Serve vegetables and some pan drippings over each hen half. Makes 4 servings.

Per Serving

Calories	399	Sodium	614 mg.
Carbohydrate	8 Gm.	Potassium	1625 mg.
Protein	13 Gm.	Cholesterol	36 mg.
Fat	34 Gm.		

Fish

The world of frozen fish is so interesting it deserves frequent experimentation. Most fish is low in fat, too, making it a wise choice.

In years past, cookbooks called for only a few varieties of fish. Today some of the time-honored favorites are less available and new species with unfamiliar names appear in freezer cases instead. Happily, it's been found that lean, white-fleshed ocean fish are interchangeable in recipes, if you allow for variations in the thickness of fillets. A recipe for sole, for instance, will work well with Greenland turbot.

As you gain experience with these new varieties you will learn that some seasonings enhance certain species, and you can adjust your recipes accordingly. But by and large substitution is safe.

Since you sometimes can't see the frozen fish you buy, it helps to know just what the lean, white-fleshed ocean fish are called. Here is a list:

Alaska pollock
Cod
Croaker
Flounder
Greenland turbot
Grouper
Haddock
Halibut

Ocean catfish
Ocean perch
Sea bass (blackfish)
Sea trout (weakfish)
Snapper
Sole
Whiting (hake)

The above fish are all available as fillets. Some are also available as steaks or simply drawn and dressed. Halibut is most commonly found in steak form.

FISH STEAKS PROVENÇAL

4 small halibut or cod steaks, 1 inch thick (2½ to 3 lbs.)
¼ cup vegetable oil
1 cup finely chopped onion
½ cup chopped green pepper
1 small clove garlic, minced
1 can (1 lb.) whole tomatoes, drained and halved

1 teaspoon Morton Lite Salt mixture
¼ teaspoon pepper
⅛ teaspoon thyme
⅛ teaspoon basil
⅛ teaspoon cayenne (optional)

If necessary, thaw steaks completely. Thoroughly dry with paper towel. Heat oil in large deep skillet over medium high heat. Add fish steaks and brown lightly, turning once, 2 to 3 minutes. Arrange in baking dish about 12″ × 7″ × 2″. Add onion, green pepper and garlic to skillet. Cook gently until tender. Stir in tomatoes, salt, pepper, thyme, basil and cayenne, and cook about 1 minute. Pour tomato mixture over fish steaks. Bake at 400° for about 15 minutes, or just until fish flakes easily with fork. Makes 8 servings.

Per Serving

Calories	257	Sodium	235 mg.
Carbohydrate	5 Gm.	Potassium	720 mg.
Protein	36 Gm.	Cholesterol	118 mg.
Fat	9 Gm.		

HALIBUT STEAK JARDINIÈRE

1 cup sliced celery
1 medium onion, sliced
1 medium green pepper, cut into ¼ inch strips (1 cup)
¼ cup vegetable oil
1 tablespoon lemon juice
½ teaspoon minced onion

1 halibut steak, 1 inch thick (about 1 lb.)
½ teaspoon Morton Lite Salt mixture
Dash pepper
1 medium tomato, peeled and sliced

Line an 8-inch-square baking dish with celery, onion and green pepper. In shallow bowl, stir together oil, lemon juice and minced onion. Sprinkle both sides of steak with salt and pepper. Dip steak in oil mixture, coating all sides. Place over vegetables in baking dish. Pour any remaining oil mixture over fish and vegetables. Arrange tomato slices on fish. Bake at 350° for 40 to 45 minutes, or just until fish flakes easily with a fork. Makes 3 servings.

Per Serving

Calories	357	Sodium	317 mg.
Carbohydrate	9 Gm.	Potassium	902 mg.
Protein	33 Gm.	Cholesterol	106 mg.
Fat	21 Gm.		

BAKED WHOLE FISH IN FOIL

1 clove garlic, minced
1 teaspoon Morton Lite Salt mixture
1 teaspoon oregano
½ teaspoon basil
½ teaspoon thyme
Dash pepper
½ cup vegetable oil

¼ cup chopped onion
1½ teaspoons grated lemon peel
¼ cup lemon juice
1 whole fish (4 to 5 lbs. dressed, with head and back fin removed)

Mix garlic, salt, herbs and pepper. Stir in oil, onion, lemon peel and juice. Tear off a sheet of heavy-duty aluminum foil twice the length of the fish plus 3 inches. Place foil in baking pan with half the piece extending over one end of the pan. Place fish on foil. Pour marinade over fish. Bring extending half of foil over fish and seal three sides with double folds. Refrigerate for 1 hour. Bake at 375° for about 45 minutes, or until fish flakes easily with fork. Makes 6 servings.

Per 6-oz. Serving

Calories	278	Sodium	190 mg.
Carbohydrate	32 Gm.	Potassium	584 mg.
Protein	15 Gm.	Cholesterol	120 mg.
Fat	1 Gm.		

STUFFED AND BAKED FISH BRUNOISE

1 whole fish (striped bass, sea bass, red snapper, lake trout, white fish), 2 to 5 lbs.
¼ cup unsalted polyunsaturated margarine
1 clove garlic, split
½ cup chopped green pepper
½ cup chopped sweet onion
¼ cup chopped celery

2 tomatoes, peeled and chopped
¼ cup chopped parsley
1 teaspoon Morton Lite Salt mixture
¼ teaspoon pepper
     * * *
Lemon or lime wedges

Have your fish dealer scale and clean the fish and remove the head. Wipe fish with damp cloth and place on a greased bake-and-serve platter. Heat margarine in skillet. Place garlic pieces on toothpicks, add to margarine and simmer gently for 5 minutes. Remove garlic. Add pepper, onion and celery and cook over moderate heat, stirring occasionally, long enough to soften (about 5 minutes). Add tomatoes, parsley, salt and pepper, and stir over low heat for 1 minute. Fill fish with as much of this stuffing as possible and arrange the rest (including liquid in pan) over and around the fish. Cover. Bake at 425° until fish flakes easily with a fork. Allow about 30 minutes for a 2- or 3-pound fish, 50 minutes for a 5-pound fish. Serve with wedges of lemon or lime. A 3-pound fish will serve 4.

Per 6-oz. Portion

Calories	240	Sodium	211 mg.
Carbohydrate	3 Gm.	Potassium	586 mg.
Protein	33 Gm.	Cholesterol	119 mg.
Fat	10 Gm.		

NEAPOLITAN FISH FILLETS

1½ lbs. fresh or frozen flounder   ⅛ teaspoon basil
    or haddock fillets   Vegetable oil
1 medium tomato, peeled and   Morton Lite Salt mixture
    chopped   Pepper
1 tablespoon minced onion

If necessary, partially thaw fillets. Preheat broiler pan and
rack for 5 minutes. Combine tomato, onion and basil; set
aside. Brush both sides of fillets with oil. Sprinkle with
salt and pepper. Place small amount of tomato mixture in
center of each fillet. Overlap both ends of fillet over
tomato; fasten with wooden picks. Arrange on broiler
rack. Broil 3 inches from source of heat, turning once and
brushing with oil, about 5 minutes on each side or until
fish flakes easily with a fork but is still moist. Makes 6
servings.

Per Serving

Calories	125	Sodium	87 mg.
Carbohydrate	1 Gm.	Potassium	383 mg.
Protein	17 Gm.	Cholesterol	56 mg.
Fat	5 Gm.		

BROILED FILLETS WITH SESAME

1 lb. fresh or frozen fish fillets   2 tablespoons sesame seeds
¼ cup unsalted polyunsatu-
    rated margarine, melted

Partially thaw fillets, if needed. Pat dry with paper towel.
Brush with melted margarine. Place on rack in broiler
pan. Sprinkle with sesame. Broil 4 inches from heat
source, basting occasionally with melted margarine, 5 to 7
minutes or until fish is tender and flakes easily when
tested with fork. Makes 3 servings.

Per Serving

Calories	363	Sodium	102 mg.
Carbohydrate	4 Gm.	Potassium	466 mg.
Protein	26 Gm.	Cholesterol	85 mg.
Fat	28 Gm.		

SOLE AMANDINE WITH TOMATOES

½ cup flour
1½ teaspoons Morton Lite Salt mixture
⅜ teaspoon pepper
1 lb. sole or flounder fillets
5 tablespoons unsalted polyunsaturated margarine

4 cups chopped, peeled tomatoes (3 to 4 large)
½ clove garlic, minced
½ teaspoon tarragon

* * *

¼ cup slivered, toasted, blanched almonds

Mix together flour, 1 teaspoon of the salt and ¼ teaspoon of the pepper, and coat fillets with this mixture. Melt 4 tablespoons of the margarine in a skillet over low heat. Add fillets; fry for 2 to 3 minutes on each side until golden brown. Keep hot. Meantime, in another skillet, melt remaining tablespoon of margarine. Add tomatoes, garlic, the remaining ½ teaspoon of salt, tarragon and the remaining ⅛ teaspoon of pepper. Cover. Cook over low heat for 2 to 3 minutes, or until tomatoes are heated through. Drain. Arrange tomato mixture on shallow platter. Place fillets on top. Garnish with almonds. Makes 4 servings.

Per Serving

Calories	354	Sodium	484 mg.
Carbohydrate	21 Gm.	Potassium	1022 mg.
Protein	22 Gm.	Cholesterol	57 mg.
Fat	22 Gm.		

ITALIAN BROILED FILLETS

1 lb. fish fillets, fresh or frozen
¼ cup unsalted polyunsaturated margarine, softened
1 tablespoon lemon juice
¼ teaspoon Morton Lite Salt mixture

Dash pepper
½ teaspoon crushed, dried mint leaves
½ teaspoon crushed oregano
Paprika

Partially thaw fillets, if necessary. Arrange fish fillets on greased broiler pan. Blend margarine with lemon juice, salt, pepper, mint and oregano. Spread mixture on fish fillets. Broil in preheated broiler 3 inches from source of heat for 3 to 5 minutes, or until fish flakes easily when tested with a fork. Sprinkle with paprika. Makes 4 servings.

Per Serving

Calories	186	Sodium	134 mg.
Carbohydrate	trace	Potassium	487 mg.
Protein	16 Gm.	Cholesterol	56 mg.
Fat	12 Gm.		

SOLE TOMATE

1½ lbs. sole fillets
1 cup coarsely chopped, peeled tomatoes
½ cup white wine
2 tablespoons flour

2 tablespoons unsalted polyunsaturated margarine
½ teaspoon Morton Lite Salt mixture
¼ teaspoon white pepper
2 tablespoons white wine

Partially thaw fillets if necessary. Arrange in skillet and top with ¾ cup of the tomatoes and ½ cup of wine. Poach, covered, over medium heat until fish flakes easily with a fork (10 to 15 minutes). Remove fish to warm platter. Strain liquid into bowl; discard tomatoes. In same skillet or small saucepan, blend flour into melted margarine. Slowly stir liquid from fish into this mixture. Add salt and pepper; stir until sauce is smooth. Bring just to a boil; reduce heat as low as possible. Stir in remaining 2 tablespoons of wine and the remaining ¼ cup of chopped tomatoes. Replace fish in sauce. Bring just to a simmer. Serve at once. Makes 6 servings.

Per Serving

Calories	150	Sodium	157 mg.
Carbohydrate	4 Gm.	Potassium	549 mg.
Protein	17 Gm.	Cholesterol	56 mg.
Fat	4 Gm.		

GRILLED LAKE SUPERIOR WHITEFISH,
MAÎTRE D'HOTEL

¼ cup unsalted polyunsaturated margarine, melted
⅛ teaspoon Morton Lite Salt mixture
Dash pepper

1 whitefish (2 lbs.), cleaned, boned and split lengthwise
1 tablespoon finely chopped parsley
1 teaspoon lemon juice

Grease broiling rack with a little melted margarine. Stir salt and pepper into remaining margarine. Brush insides of whitefish with some of this mixture. Place split fish, skin side up, on broiler rack. Brush skin generously with some of the melted margarine. Reserve remainder. Broil fish under preheated broiler 3 to 4 inches from source of heat for about 10 minutes, or until fish flakes easily with a fork. Place on serving platter. Stir chopped parsley and lemon juice into remaining margarine; pour over fish. Makes 3 servings.

Per Serving

Calories	352	Sodium	117 mg.
Carbohydrate	trace	Potassium	850 mg.
Protein	25 Gm.	Cholesterol	93 mg.
Fat	27 Gm.		

SIERRA MOUNTAIN TROUT SAUTÉ

4 to 6 ready-to-cook whole
trout, fresh or frozen
Morton Lite Salt mixture
Pepper
⅓ cup cornmeal
Vegetable oil
½ cup unsalted polyunsaturated margarine

¼ cup lemon juice
2 tablespoons sauterne or orange juice
¼ cup minced parsley
2 tablespoons chervil

* * *

Lemon wedges

Thaw trout if frozen. Season with salt and pepper and coat on all sides with cornmeal. Fry in ⅛ inch of hot oil for about 7 minutes on each side, or until fish flakes easily with a fork. Transfer to platter; keep warm. In another skillet, melt margarine and heat until bubbling. Add lemon juice and wine. Bring to a boil. Let bubble for 1 minute. Stir in parsley and chervil. Pour over trout; serve garnished with lemon wedges. Makes 6 servings.

Per Serving

Calories	383	Sodium	95 mg.
Carbohydrate	5 Gm.	Potassium	3100 mg.
Protein	12 Gm.	Cholesterol	46 mg.
Fat	35 Gm.		

Main Dish Sauces

The sauces which follow add variety to otherwise every-day foods. Each has several uses.

SWEET AND SOUR DUCK SAUCE

¼ teaspoon dry mustard
¼ teaspoon warm water
2 teaspoons cornstarch
¼ cup cold water
1 jar (10 oz.) peach or apricot preserves

1 tablespoon white vinegar
½ teaspoon ground ginger
⅛ teaspoon Morton Lite Salt mixture
Pinch ground cloves
Pinch ground red pepper

In a cup, mix mustard with warm water and let stand for 10 minutes to develop flavor. In a small saucepan, blend cornstarch with cold water. Stir in preserves, vinegar, spices and mustard. Mix well. Bring to boiling point. Reduce heat and simmer for 2 minutes, stirring constantly. Use as a glaze for duck, chicken, roast pork or spareribs, or as a sauce for Chinese foods. Makes 1 cup.

Per Recipe

Calories	1071	Sodium	203 mg.
Carbohydrate	273 Gm.	Potassium	320 mg.
Protein	3 Gm.	Cholesterol	0
Fat	3 Gm.		

HOT BARBECUE SAUCE

2 tablespoons instant minced onion
¼ teaspoon instant minced garlic
2 tablespoons water
2 tablespoons vegetable oil
1 cup homemade chicken broth
1 can (8 oz.) tomato sauce
1 can (6 oz.) tomato paste
3 tablespoons vinegar
2 tablespoons dark brown sugar
2 tablespoons parsley flakes
½ teaspoon ground allspice
¼ teaspoon Morton Lite Salt mixture
¼ teaspoon ground red pepper

Mix onion and garlic with water; let stand for 10 minutes. In a medium saucepan, heat oil. Add onion and garlic; cook for 4 minutes, or until golden. Remove from heat. Add remaining ingredients. Simmer, uncovered, for 15 minutes, stirring occasionally. Use as a basting sauce for chicken, pork chops, spareribs or fish. Makes about 2¼ cups.

Per Recipe

Calories	776	Sodium	768 mg.
Carbohydrate	73 Gm.	Potassium	2400 mg.
Protein	10 Gm.	Cholesterol	10 mg.
Fat	52 Gm.		

SWEET CATSUP SAUCE

1 piece (3 inch) stick
  cinnamon
1 teaspoon whole cloves
1 large garlic clove, chopped
1 cup vinegar
1 can (1 lb. 13 oz.) tomato
  purée

⅓ cup sugar
1¼ teaspoons Morton Lite
  Salt mixture
1 teaspoon paprika
Dash cayenne pepper

Tie cinnamon, cloves and garlic into a cheesecloth bag. Add to vinegar and simmer over low heat for 15 minutes. Meantime, place tomato purée in deep saucepan. Heat to boiling, then reduce heat until purée is plopping gently. Cook for 15 minutes, stirring frequently. Remove spices from vinegar, pressing out liquid from bag. Turn tomato purée into reduced spiced vinegar and stir to blend. Add sugar, salt, paprika and pepper. Continue cooking and stirring about 12 minutes more. Store covered in refrigerator. Use to top hamburgers, as a flavoring for baked beans or as a barbecue sauce. Makes 2 cups.

Per Recipe

Calories	434	Sodium	2878 mg.
Carbohydrate	113 Gm.	Potassium	2628 mg.
Protein	6 Gm.	Cholesterol	0
Fat	1 Gm.		

CRANBERRY GLAZE

1 cup cranberry juice cocktail
1 cup whole cranberry sauce
¼ cup honey
½ cup light corn syrup
¼ cup unsalted polyunsaturated margarine

In small saucepan, cook cranberry juice and sauce until sauce melts. Add remaining ingredients. Simmer for 10 minutes. Use as basting sauce for chicken or turkey during last 45 minutes of cooking. Makes about 2 cups.

Per Recipe

Calories	1613	Sodium	9 mg.
Carbohydrate	303 Gm.	Potassium	80 mg.
Protein	trace	Cholesterol	0
Fat	50 Gm.		

HOT MUSTARD SAUCE, DIJON STYLE

¼ cup dry mustard
¼ cup water
¼ cup vegetable oil
2 teaspoons wine
2 tablespoons mayonnaise
2 teaspoons vinegar
2 teaspoons flour
1 teaspoon sugar
½ teaspoon Morton Lite Salt mixture

Combine all ingredients; mix well. Let stand about 10 minutes before using. Store in refrigerator. Good with cold meats. Makes about ¾ cup.

Per Recipe

Calories	596	Sodium	1330 mg.
Carbohydrate	13 Gm.	Potassium	900 mg.
Protein	4 Gm.	Cholesterol	0
Fat	61 Gm.		

CHAPTER 5

THE VEGETABLES YOU COOK

CHAPTER 5

THE VEGETABLES YOU COOK

If you are seeking to improve your eating habits you will soon learn that cooked vegetables are dear friends. Most are low in calories. They contain no saturated fat, and there are many imaginative ways to dress them up without adding butter or cream. Interesting vegetable dishes and a wide variety of vegetables make menus sparkle.

Many of us like our vegetables in their simplest form and the following pages give you some good ways to achieve this. But you will also want to try some of the fancier recipes—for company, or just as an extra surprise for the family.

A Low-Water Way to Cook Frozen Vegetables

If you have a saucepan or a skillet with a tight-fitting lid, try cooking frozen vegetables by the following method to preserve flavor and "season" vegetables without adding margarine.

In saucepan, place 1 tablespoon of vegetable oil. Add a 9- or 10-ounce package of frozen vegetables and 3 tablespoons of water. Sprinkle with Morton Lite Salt mixture and pepper to taste. Cover and place over medium-low heat. After 2 minutes, break up vegetables with a fork. Shake the pan from time to time to prevent sticking. Cook until tender.

Frozen corn cooks in about 11 minutes, Italian green beans in 17 minutes, cut green beans and frozen cauliflower in 13 minutes. If you like, you may add chopped onion, chopped peeled tomato, sliced canned water chestnuts, chopped pimiento or a desired herb.

"Panned" Fresh Vegetables

The preceding method may be followed with certain fresh vegetables, too. Wash the vegetables but do not dry. For a 1-pound quantity of vegetables, follow these timing directions:

Broccoli, cauliflower, Brussels sprouts or cut green beans: 8 to 16 minutes.

Peas and cubed turnips: 23 minutes.

Check vegetables during cooking; sometimes a little more water should be added.

ASPARAGUS

Choose asparagus which is firm and unblemished. You may prefer large stiff stalks or delicate thin ones, but strive for uniform size so cooking time is the same. Hold each stalk in two hands and snap off the white butt end right around the place it starts to turn green; discard the butt, or use in soups. Wash remaining stalks thoroughly in several changes of lukewarm water. Stalks may be set upright in an asparagus cooker or laid flat in a skillet. Add a small amount (about ½ inch) of boiling water and ½ teaspoon of Morton Lite Salt mixture. Cover and cook for 10 to 20 minutes, or until butt ends are tender. One pound serves 3.

Per Serving

Calories	39	Sodium	186 mg.
Carbohydrate	8 Gm.	Potassium	312 mg.
Protein	4 Gm.	Cholesterol	0
Fat	trace		

ASPARAGUS POLONAISE

2 lb. cooked asparagus
¼ lb. unsalted polyunsaturated margarine
⅔ cup freshly made bread crumbs

1 hard-cooked egg
Juice of 1 lemon
2 tablespoons chopped parsley

Just before asparagus is cooked, melt margarine; add bread crumbs and sauté until golden. Sieve egg yolk and white separately. Place drained asparagus on hot platter. Sprinkle with lemon juice, browned crumbs, sieved egg and parsley. Makes 6 servings.

Per Serving

Calories	228	Sodium	87 mg.
Carbohydrate	15 Gm.	Potassium	80 mg.
Protein	6 Gm.	Cholesterol	44 mg.
Fat	17 Gm.		

GREEN BEANS

Select unblemished crisp fresh beans. With fingers, snap off ends and wash. Beans may be cooked this way or broken or cut into pieces 1½ inches long. To cut beans French-style, place on cutting board and cut on deep diagonal, about ½ inch apart, so much of the bean's interior is exposed.

Place the beans in a heavy saucepan with 1 inch of boiling water. Add ½ teaspoon of Morton Lite Salt mixture per pound. Cover and cook for 15 minutes for French-cut beans, about 25 minutes for whole green beans. Drain. Add unsalted polyunsaturated margarine to taste. One pound serves 4.

Per Serving

Calories	36	Sodium	145 mg.
Carbohydrate	8 Gm.	Potassium	238 mg.
Protein	2 Gm.	Cholesterol	0
Fat	trace		

ITALIAN-STYLE GREEN BEANS

1 tablespoon instant minced onion
¼ teaspoon instant minced garlic
2 tablespoons water
2 tablespoons vegetable oil

2 packages (9 oz. each) frozen cut green beans
1 teaspoon basil
1 teaspoon Morton Lite Salt mixture
⅛ teaspoon pepper

Mix minced onion and garlic with 1 tablespoon of water and let stand for 10 minutes. In a large skillet, heat oil. Add onion and garlic; sauté for 5 minutes. Reduce heat; add green beans, basil, salt, pepper and remaining tablespoon of water. Cover and simmer for 5 to 8 minutes, or until beans are crisp-tender, stirring occasionally. Check frequently so beans don't burn. Makes 6 servings.

Per Serving

Calories	63	Sodium	184 mg.
Carbohydrate	5 Gm.	Potassium	303 mg.
Protein	1 Gm.	Cholesterol	0
Fat	5 Gm.		

DILLY BEANS AND CARROTS

½ lb. fresh green beans
4 medium-sized carrots
¾ cup water
1 teaspoon sugar

½ teaspoon Morton Lite Salt mixture
½ teaspoon dill seed

* * *

¼ cup Basic French Dressing (page 139)

Wash, trim and slice green beans. Cut carrots into thin strips 2 to 3 inches long. Combine water, sugar, salt and dill seed in a saucepan; bring to boil. Add carrots and green beans, cover, and simmer for 5 minutes. Boil until both vegetables are tender and liquid is almost evaporated (about 10 minutes). Add dressing and toss. Serve hot, or chill and use in tossed vegetable salad. Makes 6 servings.

Per Serving

Calories	30	Sodium	116 mg.
Carbohydrate	7 Gm.	Potassium	266 mg.
Protein	1 Gm.	Cholesterol	0
Fat	trace		

BROCCOLI

The best broccoli is dark green, sage green or purple green, with short stems, small leaves and compact buds. Avoid broccoli which shows yellowing or open blossoms. Remove the leaves and cut off tough stalk ends. Soak in cold water containing 2 tablespoons of Morton Lite Salt mixture for 30 minutes. Drain and rinse. Peel off the skin from the main stalks, but leave it on the branches. Make crosswise cuts about 2 inches deep in large stalks. Place in saucepan with 2 inches of boiling water and 1 teaspoon of Morton Lite Salt mixture. Without covering, cook for 3 minutes. Cover and cook for 8 to 18 minutes more, or until stalks are tender. Drain. Sprinkle with lemon juice or top with unsalted polyunsaturated margarine. One pound serves 3.

Calories	48	Sodium	389 mg.
Carbohydrate	9 Gm.	Potassium	600 mg.
Protein	5 Gm.	Cholesterol	0
Fat	trace		

BROCCOLI FLORENTINE

2 packages (10 oz. each) frozen chopped spinach
¾ cup boiling water
1¼ teaspoons Morton Lite Salt mixture

⅓ cup half-and-half
¼ cup sliced green onions
1 package (10 oz.) frozen broccoli spears

Crumb Topping:

¼ cup dry bread crumbs
¼ teaspoon Morton Lite Salt mixture

¼ teaspoon nutmeg
Few grains cayenne pepper
1 tablespoon vegetable oil

Cook spinach in ½ cup of boiling water with ½ teaspoon salt for 20 minutes. Drain well. In buttered, shallow 1½-quart casserole, mix together cooked spinach, half-and-half, green onions and ½ teaspoon of salt. Set aside.

Cook broccoli in ¼ cup of boiling water with ¼ teaspoon salt for about 8 minutes, or until tender. Arrange broccoli spears over top of spinach mixture. (This much may be done ahead and refrigerated until shortly before serving.)

To make Crumb Topping: In a small bowl, combine crumbs, salt, nutmeg and cayenne. Mix well. Add oil, mix to moisten all the crumbs. Sprinkle over broccoli. Bake at 400° for 5 minutes (if at room temperature), for 10 to 15 minutes (if chilled), just until spinach bubbles and topping is browned. Makes 6 servings.

Per Serving

Calories	71	Sodium	368 mg.
Carbohydrate	10 Gm.	Potassium	626 mg.
Protein	5 Gm.	Cholesterol	7 mg.
Fat	2 Gm.		

BRUSSELS SPROUTS

Choose firm, solid, round heads with compact leaves and a fresh green color. Avoid yellow mottling. Cut off stem ends and remove wilted leaves. Cut a gash in each stem. Soak in water containing 2 tablespoons of Morton Lite Salt mixture for 30 minutes. Drain and rinse. Place in saucepan with 1 inch of boiling water containing ½ teaspoon of Morton Lite Salt mixture per pound. Without covering, cook for 3 minutes. Cover and cook for 8 to 15 minutes more. Drain. Serve with unsalted polyunsaturated margarine and lemon juice. One quart of sprouts serves 6.

Per Serving

Calories	34	Sodium	102 mg.
Carbohydrate	6 Gm.	Potassium	300 mg.
Protein	3 Gm.	Cholesterol	0
Fat	trace		

BRUSSELS SPROUTS AMANDINE

Cook 1 pint of sprouts as above. During the last 10 minutes of cooking, melt 2 tablespoons of unsalted polyunsaturated margarine in a heavy pan. Add ½ cup of shredded blanched almonds and shake over low heat until lightly browned. Drain sprouts, put in serving dish and top with almond mixture. If desired, sprinkle with a few drops of lemon juice. Makes 4 servings.

Per Serving

Calories	193	Sodium	9 mg.
Carbohydrate	9 Gm.	Potassium	400 mg.
Protein	7 Gm.	Cholesterol	0
Fat	18 Gm.		

CABBAGE

Choose a solid head, heavy for its size, with fresh leaves. Remove damaged outer leaves. Submerge in water and wash thoroughly. (If desired, add 2 tablespoons of Morton Lite Salt mixture to water.) To cook, cut into 6 to 8 wedges. Place in saucepan with 1 inch of boiling water and 1 teaspoon of Morton Lite Salt mixture. Cover and boil rapidly for 10 to 15 minutes, lifting cover from time to time. Or, for shredded cabbage, cut into thin strips with sharp French chef's knife or grater. Place in saucepan with 1 inch of boiling water and 1 teaspoon of Morton Lite Salt mixture. Cover and cook for 8 to 10 minutes or until tender. Drain. Add unsalted polyunsaturated margarine. Or dress with a small amount of vinegar. One pound serves 4.

Per Serving

Calories	27	Sodium	297 mg.
Carbohydrate	6 Gm.	Potassium	100 mg.
Protein	1 Gm.	Cholesterol	0
Fat	trace		

CHINESE-STYLE CABBAGE

3 tablespoons vegetable oil
5 cups (about 1 lb.) shredded cabbage
2 tablespoons sugar
1 teaspoon Morton Lite Salt mixture
Dash pepper
1 tablespoon white vinegar

Use a wok (a Chinese cooking pan), an electric skillet set to high, or a conventional skillet over high heat. Place oil in pan and heat. Add cabbage and reduce heat to moderate. Cook for 3 minutes, tossing and turning cabbage constantly. Add sugar, salt, pepper and vinegar. Cook, stirring constantly, until cabbage is crisp-tender (about 3 minutes). Reduce heat, cover and simmer for another 3 minutes. Makes 4 servings.

Per Serving

Calories	148	Sodium	300 mg.
Carbohydrate	13 Gm.	Potassium	450 mg.
Protein	2 Gm.	Cholesterol	0
Fat	11 Gm.		

SPICED RED CABBAGE

¼ cup unsalted polyunsaturated margarine
3 cooking apples, pared, cored and cubed
¼ cup chopped onion
1 medium head red cabbage, finely shredded

1 tablespoon sugar
½ teaspoon Morton Lite Salt mixture
2 whole cloves
2 bay leaves
Dash cinnamon
1½ cups water
½ cup vinegar

Melt margarine in large saucepan. Add apples and onion; cook over low heat, stirring frequently, until onion is lightly browned. Add cabbage; toss lightly and cook until cabbage looks wilted. Combine remaining ingredients and stir into cabbage mixture. Cover; simmer, stirring occasionally, until cabbage is tender, 1 to 2 hours. Makes 1½ quarts, 6 servings.

Per Serving

Calories	139	Sodium	103 mg.
Carbohydrate	17 Gm.	Potassium	333 mg.
Protein	1 Gm.	Cholesterol	0
Fat	9 Gm.		

CARROTS

Carrots will keep fresh longer if tops are removed. For cooking, carrots may range from midget size (2 to 3 inches in length) to full size. Very large carrots may be woody and are best used cut up in stews and soups. Cut off stem end and scrape with vegetable peeler. Wash. Leave tiny carrots whole. Cut others into julienne strips or pennies. Place in saucepan with 1 inch of water and 1 teaspoon of Morton Lite Salt mixture. Cover and cook for 15 to 25 minutes for young whole carrots or 10 to 20 minutes for sliced carrots, or until just tender. Serve with unsalted polyunsaturated margarine, chopped parsley or chopped fresh mint. One pound serves 4.

Per Serving

Calories	47	Sodium	328 mg.
Carbohydrate	11 Gm.	Potassium	275 mg.
Protein	1 Gm.	Cholesterol	0
Fat	trace		

CAULIFLOWER

Choose an all-white, tightly packed head without wilted spots or bruises. Remove leaves and cut off stem.

Whole Cauliflower: Submerge in cold water containing 2 tablespoons of Morton Lite Salt mixture and soak for 30 minutes. Drain and rinse. Place in saucepan with 2 inches of boiling water. Cook for 15 to 20 minutes, or until tender, lifting cover from time to time. Drain well and season as desired with unsalted polyunsaturated margarine. A 2-pound head serves 6.

Cauliflowerets: Break and cut cauliflower into pieces about 1½ inches in diameter. Wash. Place in a saucepan with 1 inch of boiling water containing 1 teaspoon of Morton Lite Salt mixture. Cover and cook for 8 to 15 minutes, until tender, lifting cover once during cooking. Season as desired. A 2-pound head serves 6.

Cauliflower Cues: Among spices which taste good on cauliflower are caraway seed, dill weed, mace and tarragon. A sprinkling of paprika when ready to serve enhances both flavor and appearance.

Per Serving

Calories	36	Sodium	201 mg.
Carbohydrate	7 Gm.	Potassium	200 mg.
Protein	4 Gm.	Cholesterol	0
Fat	trace		

CORN

The tastiest corn is just picked, with well-filled ears and fresh green husks. Remove husks and all silk. In a large kettle, heat to boiling enough water to cover corn (5 to 6 inches). Add 2 teaspoons of Morton Lite Salt mixture and 1 teaspoon of sugar. Add corn and cook for 5 to 15 minutes, until tender. Remove from water with tongs. Serve as is with unsalted polyunsaturated margarine and Morton Lite Salt mixture, or cut from cob and toss with margarine and salt. Appetites for corn vary—count on 1½ ears per person.

Calories	149	Sodium	733 mg.
Carbohydrate	34 Gm.	Potassium	233 mg.
Protein	5 Gm.	Cholesterol	0
Fat	1 Gm.		

CURRIED CORN

¼ cup unsalted polyunsatu-   ¼ teaspoon curry powder
rated margarine

Cream margarine and curry together. Pass with hot ears of corn—recipe will be sufficient for 6 ears. Or cut corn off cob and toss mixture with kernels. Enough for 3 cups.

Per Serving

Calories	202	Sodium	551 mg.
Carbohydrate	34 Gm.	Potassium	233 mg.
Protein	5 Gm.	Cholesterol	0
Fat	8 Gm.		

MEXICAN STYLE CORN

2 tablespoons unsalted polyun-   2 cups (¾ lb.) sliced summer
saturated margarine   squash
⅓ cup finely chopped onion   ½ teaspoon Morton Lite Salt
4 ears fresh corn, cut off the   mixture
cob   ¼ teaspoon freshly ground pep-
3 cups diced, peeled fresh   per
tomatoes

Melt margarine in a skillet. Add remaining ingredients; cover and cook for 10 to 15 minutes, or until squash is tender. Cook for an additional 15 minutes, uncovered. Makes 6 servings.

Per Serving

Calories	142	Sodium	98 mg.
Carbohydrate	23 Gm.	Potassium	200 mg.
Protein	4 Gm.	Cholesterol	0
Fat	5 Gm.		

EGGPLANT

Choose hard, firm eggplant with smooth, shiny skin, heavy for its size. Wash and pare. Cut in ½-inch-thick slices. If boiled eggplant is desired, place in 1 inch of boiling water with 1 teaspoon of Morton Lite Salt mixture. Cover and cook for 10 to 20 minutes. It is more commonly fried. Sprinkle slices with salt and pepper. Dip into beaten egg, then fine dry bread crumbs. Brown on both sides in hot vegetable oil. Drain on absorbent paper. A medium-size eggplant serves 6.

Per Serving (Boiled Eggplant)

Calories	28	Sodium	186 mg.
Carbohydrate	7 Gm.	Potassium	200 mg.
Protein	1 Gm.	Cholesterol	0
Fat	trace		

EGGPLANT-TOMATO CASSEROLE

1 large onion, chopped
2 small eggplants, peeled and diced
¼ cup unsalted polyunsaturated margarine

1 can (28 oz.) tomatoes, drained and cut up*
1 teaspoon Morton Lite Salt mixture
Dash pepper
¼ cup corn flake crumbs

Cook onion and eggplant in margarine until golden brown. Add tomatoes, salt and pepper. Mix thoroughly. Pour into casserole and top with crumbs. Bake at 350° for 30 minutes. Makes 6 servings.

*Or use 5 medium (1½ lbs.) tomatoes, peeled, cored and cut up.

Per Serving

Calories	109	Sodium	190 mg.
Carbohydrate	8 Gm.	Potassium	700 mg.
Protein	2 Gm.	Cholesterol	0
Fat	9 Gm.		

MUSHROOMS

Look for white or creamy mushrooms without blemishes and with a velvety-looking surface. Keep them refrigerated when not in use, and wash only those you plan to use at once. Spray-wash, or dip briefly into a basin of cold water. Don't peel mushrooms. You will probably want to remove the last quarter-inch of the stem, which is often dried looking, and cut away any blemishes. When stewing mushrooms, leave smaller ones whole, slice larger ones. Place in a small amount of boiling water with ½ teaspoon of Morton Lite Salt mixture per pound. Cover and simmer for 5 to 10 minutes. If desired, first cook mushrooms gently in unsalted polyunsaturated margarine for 5 minutes, then add ¼ cup of water, cover and simmer 3 minutes more. One pound serves 5.

Per Serving

Calories	25	Sodium	123 mg.
Carbohydrate	4 Gm.	Potassium	350 mg.
Protein	2 Gm.	Cholesterol	0
Fat	trace		

SAUTÉED MUSHROOMS

1 lb. fresh mushrooms	¼ cup unsalted polyunsaturated
4 cups cold water	margarine, melted
1 tablespoon lemon juice	Morton Lite Salt mixture
	White pepper

Trim stem ends of mushrooms, rinse, then soak in cold water and lemon juice for 5 minutes. Drain and pat dry. Sauté in margarine sprinkled with salt and pepper, until lightly browned, turning occasionally. Makes 6 servings.

Per Serving

Calories	91	Sodium	57 mg.
Carbohydrate	3 Gm.	Potassium	333 mg.
Protein	2 Gm.	Cholesterol	0
Fat	9 Gm.		

CURRIED MUSHROOMS

½ lb. fresh mushrooms
¼ cup unsalted polyunsaturated
  margarine
¾ cup minced onion
1 small clove garlic, crushed
1 teaspoon curry powder

⅓ cup homemade beef broth
  or water
¼ teaspoon Morton Lite Salt
  mixture

* * *

Cooked rice or noodles

Rinse mushrooms and pat dry. Slice to make about 2½ cups. In a medium saucepan, heat margarine. Add mushrooms and onion, and sauté until lightly browned (about 5 minutes), stirring occasionally. Add garlic and curry powder; cook 2 minutes longer, or until curry powder darkens. Add broth or water and salt. Reduce heat; simmer for 8 to 10 minutes. Serve over cooked rice or noodles, if desired. Makes 4 servings.

Per Serving

Calories	137	Sodium	81 mg.
Carbohydrate	6 Gm.	Potassium	450 mg.
Protein	2 Gm.	Cholesterol	0
Fat	13 Gm.		

PARSNIPS

Choose firm, well-shaped, small to medium parsnips. Wash and scrape with vegetable peeler. Cut into sticks or slices. Place in boiling water to cover with 1 teaspoon of Morton Lite Salt mixture per pound. Cover and cook about 20 minutes, or until tender. Drain and add unsalted polyunsaturated margarine. If desired, mash or sauté. One pound serves 4.

Per Serving

Calories	103	Sodium	289 mg.
Carbohydrate	20 Gm.	Potassium	450 mg.
Protein	2 Gm.	Cholesterol	0
Fat	3 Gm.		

Most produce departments offer at least three kinds of onions. Large Spanish or Bermuda onions are mild in flavor, good for salads and also for stuffing. Smaller yellow onions are used chopped or sliced in cooking. Dainty white onions are often cooked and served whole. Onions should have a hard, dry skin and look firm. They should not be sprouted. To prepare boiled onions, first peel them. (You may do this under cold water to save tears.) Place in a large amount of boiling water with 1 teaspoon of Morton Lite Salt mixture per pound. Boil uncovered for 20 to 40 minutes, or until tender but not falling apart. Drain, season and add unsalted polyunsaturated margarine. Or mix with white sauce. One pound serves 4.

Per Serving

Calories	61	Sodium	287 mg.
Carbohydrate	10 Gm.	Potassium	200 mg.
Protein	2 Gm.	Cholesterol	0
Fat	2 Gm.		

GLAZED ONIONS

Cook 1½ pounds of small white onions following directions above. Melt ⅓ cup unsalted polyunsaturated margarine in a large skillet. Add drained onions and 2 tablespoons of sugar. Cook over low heat, stirring occasionally, until golden brown (about 15 minutes). Makes 6 servings.

Per Serving

Calories	176	Sodium	195 mg.
Carbohydrate	14 Gm.	Potassium	200 mg.
Protein	2 Gm.	Cholesterol	0
Fat	13 Gm.		

GREEN PEAS

Choose fresh, unspotted green pods. If you have never shelled peas, examine the pod. You will find that one edge yields easily to finger pressure, opening almost as efficiently as a zipper. With your thumb, open pods, then shoot out peas into a saucepan as though you were shooting a marble. Wash briefly. Place in saucepan with 1 inch of water and ½ teaspoon of Morton Lite Salt mixture per pound of peas in the shell. Cover; cook for 8 to 20 minutes, or until average-size pea is tender. Drain; season with unsalted polyunsaturated margarine. Two pounds of peas in the pod serves 4.

Per Serving

Calories	112	Sodium	140 mg.
Carbohydrate	16 Gm.	Potassium	225 mg.
Protein	7 Gm.	Cholesterol	0
Fat	2 Gm.		

GREEN PEAS À LA FRANÇAISE

6 to 8 large, moist lettuce leaves
2 cups shelled peas
3 green onions
2 tablespoons minced celery leaves
1 teaspoon sugar
½ teaspoon Morton Lite Salt mixture
Dash of pepper
¼ cup boiling water
2 tablespoons unsalted polyunsaturated margarine

Line the bottom of a heavy skillet with 3 to 4 lettuce leaves. Add peas. Thinly slice the white part of the green onions and add with remaining ingredients, distributing over peas. Cover peas with remaining lettuce leaves. Cook, covered, over low heat for 5 to 7 minutes, or until tender. Discard lettuce leaves. Add margarine; cover pan and shake to distribute contents. Make 4 servings.

Per Serving

Calories	121	Sodium	140 mg.
Carbohydrate	12 Gm.	Potassium	300 mg.
Protein	4 Gm.	Cholesterol	0
Fat	6 Gm.		

POTATOES

Since most potatoes are sold packaged, you must depend on the conscience and luck of your grocer rather than your eye to select potatoes. They should be unblemished, fairly regular in shape and size and fairly clean, with shallow eyes. *Regular* potatoes may be used for boiling, mashing and frying. *Baking* potatoes are the best type for baking. *New* potatoes are a little waxy when cooked. They are delicious boiled in their jackets and served with chopped parsley and melted unsalted polyunsaturated margarine. They also make excellent potato salad.

BOILED POTATOES

If potatoes are to be cooked in their jackets, scrub well with a vegetable brush in several changes of water. Remove eyes with the tip of a vegetable peeler. Or peel and remove discolored portions and eyes, then wash well. Place in a saucepan with 2 inches of boiling water and 1 teaspoon of Morton Lite Salt mixture per pound. Cover and cook for 25 to 40 minutes for whole medium regular potatoes or small new potatoes, or about 20 minutes for quartered regular potatoes. Drain well, then shake pan over low heat until potatoes are dry and mealy. One pound serves 3.

Per Serving

Calories	114	Sodium	371 mg.
Carbohydrate	26 Gm.	Potassium	600 mg.
Protein	3 Gm.	Cholesterol	0
Fat	trace		

MASHED POTATOES

After potatoes are boiled until tender, mash thoroughly over low heat. Beat in 2 tablespoons of unsalted polyunsaturated margarine for each pound. If necessary, add a small amount of skim milk and beat until desired consistency. Serves 4.

Per Serving

Calories	145	Sodium	287 mg.
Carbohydrate	20 Gm.	Potassium	450 mg.
Protein	3 Gm.	Cholesterol	trace
Fat	6 Gm.		

BAKED POTATOES

Select baking potatoes. Wash under running water, scrubbing with a vegetable brush. Pat dry with paper towel. Rub skins with vegetable oil or unsalted polyunsaturated margarine. Place in a baking pan and bake at 450° for 45 minutes or at 350° for 1 hour and 15 minutes. To test doneness, squeeze gently, protecting your hand with several layers of paper towel. Make crosswise cuts in top and press sides of potato to "mash" and force a little of the potato up through the cuts. Serve with unsalted polyunsaturated margarine. The typical serving is one baked potato per person, but two dieters may want to share one potato.

Per Serving

Calories	211	Sodium	7 mg.
Carbohydrate	32 Gm.	Potassium	600 mg.
Protein	4 Gm.	Cholesterol	0
Fat	8 Gm.		

BASQUE POTATOES

2 lbs. potatoes
2 teaspoons unsalted polyunsaturated margarine
½ cup chopped onion
1 clove garlic, minced

½ cup chopped celery
½ cup grated carrot
2 cups homemade beef broth
1 teaspoon Morton Lite Salt mixture
2 tablespoons chopped parsley

Peel and cut potatoes into 1-inch cubes. Cover with water and let stand while preparing sauce. Melt margarine in saucepan. Add onion, garlic, celery and carrot. Sauté until vegetables are limp. Add potatoes and mix well. Add broth and salt. Cover and simmer slowly until potatoes are tender (about 20 to 25 minutes). Sprinkle with parsley. Makes 6 servings.

Per Serving

Calories	153	Sodium	347 mg.
Carbohydrate	31 Gm.	Potassium	616 mg.
Protein	5 Gm.	Cholesterol	0
Fat	2 Gm.		

POTATOES O'BRIEN

¼ cup vegetable oil (about)
4 cups diced or sliced cooked potatoes
¼ cup finely chopped onion
¼ cup chopped green pepper

¼ cup chopped pimiento*
1 teaspoon Morton Lite Salt mixture
⅛ teaspoon pepper

Heat oil in a large skillet. Add potatoes and onion; brown on all sides over medium heat, stirring frequently, about 15 minutes. Add green pepper and pimiento and continue frying, turning and stirring for 5 minutes more. Season with salt and pepper. Makes 4 servings.

*Or use 1 jar (2 oz.) pimiento strips, drained.

Per Serving

Calories	326	Sodium	284 mg.
Carbohydrate	45 Gm.	Potassium	900 mg.
Protein	6 Gm.	Cholesterol	0
Fat	15 Gm.		

SPINACH

If you are offered "loose" fresh spinach, look for small leaves on stems which are free from dirt or sand. Leaves should be unblemished and bright dark green. Discard root ends. Wash in several changes of lukewarm water, each time lifting spinach up and out to let sand drain away. Packaged fresh spinach has root ends already removed and needs only one washing in a large amount of lukewarm water. Spinach may be cooked in only the water clinging to the leaves, but many people like it better with ½ cup of water in the bottom of the saucepan. In either case, add ½ teaspoon of Morton Lite Salt mixture to a pound of fresh spinach or 1 package of the cello-bagged variety. Cover and cook about 3 minutes, or only until compact, turning once during cooking. Turn into a strainer and slice-chop in both directions with paring knife. Turn into serving dish and season with unsalted polyunsaturated margarine. One pound serves 4.

Per Serving

Calories	47	Sodium	218 mg.
Carbohydrate	5 Gm.	Potassium	550 mg.
Protein	4 Gm.	Cholesterol	0
Fat	2 Gm.		

SUMMER SQUASH

You will find two principal varieties: yellow summer squash and its close cousin, zucchini. Both are cooked in the same way. Choose firm, well-shaped squash. Large ones are often good stuffed. For boiling or frying, smaller squash are more desirable. If you prefer the skin on the squash, wash it well with a vegetable brush. Otherwise, remove it with a vegetable peeler. Slice or dice. Place in saucepan with ½ cup of boiling water and ½ teaspoon of Morton Lite Salt mixture per pound. Cover and cook about 10 minutes, or until almost tender. Uncover and boil rapidly to evaporate excess liquid. Add unsalted polyunsaturated margarine and serve. One pound serves 4.

		Per Serving		
Calories	39	Sodium	139 mg.
Carbohydrate	5 Gm.	Potassium	400 mg.
Protein	1 Gm.	Cholesterol	0
Fat	2 Gm.		

SUMMER SQUASH, ITALIAN STYLE

Prepare squash for cooking as above, slicing it paper thin. In a saucepan, cook 2 cloves of garlic, minced in ½ cup of vegetable or olive oil, over low heat for 1 minute. Add squash and toss. Cover and cook for 10 to 15 minutes over low heat, or until squash is tender. Drain and serve. This amount of oil will dress about 1½ pounds of squash, enough for 6.

		Per Serving		
Calories	156	Sodium	290 mg.
Carbohydrate	20 Gm.	Potassium	350 mg.
Protein	4 Gm.	Cholesterol	0
Fat	7 Gm.		

PARSLIED ZUCCHINI

2 lbs. boiled zucchini
2 tablespoons unsalted polyunsaturated margarine
1 tablespoon instant minced onion
¼ teaspoon grated lemon peel
1 to 1½ tablespoons lemon juice
½ cup minced parsley

During last few minutes that zucchini is cooking, in a small saucepan, combine margarine, onion, lemon peel and juice and heat until melted. Pour over drained zucchini. Add parsley and toss as for salad to mix well. Makes 6 servings.

		Per Serving		
Calories	70	Sodium	5 mg.
Carbohydrate	8 Gm.	Potassium	266 mg.
Protein	2 Gm.	Cholesterol	0
Fat	4 Gm.		

NEAPOLITAN ZUCCHINI

1 lb. zucchini
1 lb. tomatoes, peeled and diced
1 teaspoon oregano leaves
Few grinds pepper

1 teaspoon instant minced onion
½ teaspoon garlic powder
½ teaspoon Morton Lite Salt mixture

Wash zucchini and slice crosswise into ½-inch-thick rounds. In medium-size saucepan, combine zucchini with remaining ingredients. Cook, covered, over medium heat until zucchini is tender, about 15 minutes. Makes 4 servings.

Per Serving

Calories	45	Sodium	143 mg.
Carbohydrate	10 Gm.	Potassium	575 mg.
Protein	2 Gm.	Cholesterol	0
Fat	trace		

WINTER SQUASH

Hubbard squash is a large dark green vegetable weighing 5 pounds or more. Acorn squash are smaller—about the size of grapefruit. To prepare either you will need a cutting board and a sharp sturdy knife. Use these to cut squash in half. Then, if you are dealing with a Hubbard squash, cut each half into 4 more pieces. Butternut squash, which is medium in size and like a beige-colored elongated pear, may be cut in 6 pieces.

To boil squash: Peel and discard seeds and strings. Cut into smaller pieces. Place in boiling water to cover, with ½ teaspoon of Morton Lite Salt mixture per pound. Cover and cook for 20 to 30 minutes, or until tender. If desired, mash or force through a sieve. Add unsalted polyunsaturated margarine and serve. One Hubbard squash serves 8. One acorn squash serves 2.

To bake squash: Place it skin side up in a shallow baking pan. (Grease the baking pan for acorn squash.) Bake at 400° for 30 minutes. Turn skin side down. Fill cavities with a little unsalted polyunsaturated margarine, a sprinkling of Morton Lite Salt mixture, and, if you like, a little nutmeg and brown sugar. Continue baking for 15 minutes more.

Per Average Serving (Acorn or Hubbard)

Calories	74	Sodium	139 mg.
Carbohydrate	14 Gm.	Potassium	400 mg.
Protein	2 Gm.	Cholesterol	0
Fat	2 Gm.		

BUTTERNUT SQUASH CASSEROLE

2½ lbs. butternut squash
¼ cup unsalted polyunsaturated margarine
½ cup chopped onion
2 tablespoons sugar

1 teaspoon Morton Lite Salt mixture
1½ teaspoons grated orange peel
1 teaspoon cinnamon

Wash and pare butternut squash. Cut in pieces, discarding string and seed portion. Cook in a small amount of boiling water until tender, about 15 to 20 minutes. Drain and mash. Heat margarine in medium skillet. Add onion and sauté until tender. Combine with squash and remaining ingredients. Blend well; turn into greased 1-quart casserole. Bake, uncovered, at 350° for 20 minutes. Makes about 4 servings.

Per Serving

Calories	281	Sodium	282 mg.
Carbohydrate	43 Gm.	Potassium	575 mg.
Protein	4 Gm.	Cholesterol	0
Fat	13 Gm.		

SWEET POTATOES

Sweet potatoes with light-colored skins are dry and mealy. If the skin is deeper orange or reddish, the vegetable is sweeter and more moist. The skin should be firm and smooth, without soft spots or discoloration or shriveling at the root end. To boil sweet potatoes, scrub them perfectly clean with a vegetable brush and trim off roots. Place in saucepan with boiling water to cover. Cover and cook for 25 to 35 minutes, or until fork-tender. Drain and peel. Sweet potatoes are appetizing served whole, surrounding a roast chicken or loin of pork. They may also be mashed like white potatoes. One pound serves 3.

BAKED SWEET POTATOES

Wash sweet potatoes thoroughly, using a vegetable brush. Pat dry, then rub with oil or soft unsalted polyunsaturated margarine. Place in baking pan in oven and bake at 400° for 30 to 40 minutes, or until fork-tender. Make crosswise cuts in top and press with paper-towel-protected fingers to force a little sweet potato through cuts.

Per Serving

Calories	211	Sodium	18 mg.
Carbohydrate	49 Gm.	Potassium	600 mg.
Protein	3 Gm.	Cholesterol	0
Fat	trace		

TOMATOES

When you are choosing tomatoes to be served raw, you must look for unblemished, firm, plump tomatoes with unspotted skin and bright color. When the tomatoes are destined to be cooked, you may be able to buy blemished ones at a considerable saving and simply cut away the unwanted parts. No matter how you plan to use them, you will wash them and cut out the stem end, removing a small cone-shaped piece. To peel tomatoes, plunge them briefly in boiling water; then skin will slip off easily.

To stew tomatoes: Peel and quarter ripe tomatoes. Put into a saucepan. Add desired seasonings; chopped onion, crumbled bay leaf or chopped celery tops may be used. For every pound of tomatoes add ½ teaspoon of Morton Lite Salt mixture and 1 teaspoon of sugar. Without adding water, cover and simmer over low heat for 5 to 15 minutes, or until soft. If the tomatoes are very juicy, mix 2 teaspoons of cornstarch with 2 tablespoons of cold water, then stir into juice. Bring to boil and cook until thickened. Makes 4 servings.

Per Serving

Calories	59	Sodium	281 mg.
Carbohydrate	13 Gm.	Potassium	575 mg.
Protein	2 Gm.	Cholesterol	0
Fat	trace		

To broil tomatoes: Cut a thin slice from the top of small tomatoes or cut larger ones in half. Sprinkle the cut surface with Morton Lite Salt mixture and freshly ground pepper. Dot with unsalted polyunsaturated margarine. Broil for 3 to 5 minutes, or until hot and lightly browned. If desired, sprinkle with fine dry bread crumbs before adding margarine. One pound serves 4.

Per Serving

Calories	51	Sodium	142 mg.
Carbohydrate	7 Gm.	Potassium	400 mg.
Protein	2 Gm.	Cholesterol	0
Fat	3 Gm.		

TURNIPS

Select either white turnips by the bunch or a yellow turnip by size. Either should be smooth, firm and heavy for its size. Small turnips should be scraped with a vegetable peeler. It is somewhat easier to pare a larger turnip if you wash it first and cut it into wedges. Leave small turnips whole; slice or dice larger ones. (When sliced thin or grated, raw turnips make an interesting addition to salads.) To boil, place in saucepan with boiling water to cover and 1 teaspoon of Morton Lite Salt mixture per pound. Boil rapidly for 15 to 20 minutes, or until fork-tender. Drain well. Mash if desired, as for white potatoes. Many people like turnips when mixed in equal proportions with mashed white potatoes. This dish may be seasoned lightly with nutmeg. One pound serves 4.

Per Serving

Calories	34	Sodium	330 mg.
Carbohydrate	7 Gm.	Potassium	600 mg.
Protein	1 Gm.	Cholesterol	0
Fat	trace		

YAMS

Good yams are plump with tapered ends and a coppery-colored skin. Scrub well, using a vegetable brush. To boil, place in a saucepan with boiling water to cover and 1 teaspoon of Morton Lite Salt mixture per pound. Cook about 30 minutes, or until tender. Slip off skins and serve with unsalted polyunsaturated margarine. Count on 1 yam for each person, although dieters may prefer ½ yam apiece.

To bake: Place in baking pan and bake at 400° for 15 minutes. Reduce heat to 375° and bake for 40 minutes more, or until tender.

Per Serving (Boiled Yams, no Margarine)

Calories	132	Sodium	284 mg.
Carbohydrate	26 Gm.	Potassium	500 mg.
Protein	2 Gm.	Cholesterol	0
Fat	2 Gm.		

CHAPTER 6

SALADS

CHAPTER 6

SALADS

Many people like a salad for lunch as well as for dinner. There are many different kinds of salads and it is reasonably easy to invent your own masterpiece.

The green salad is a classic in French menus and admirably accompanies most meats. For some families the typical salad is fruit, either fresh or canned. These salads make eating fruits and vegetables more interesting and provide a contrast in temperature to an otherwise hot meal.

Jellied salads may be made a full day in advance, an advantage to the hostess planning a complicated buffet, or to the working homemaker.

Potato and macaroni salads star in the summertime when cold meals taste so good. Special care should be taken to keep them cold at all times, since these mixtures spoil easily at room temperature.

Do find out how easy it is to make your own salad dressing, using good vegetable oil and Morton Lite Salt mixture. The flavor will be fresh and you can personalize recipes with your own seasoning blend.

GOOD GREEN SALAD

An excellent green salad sets off almost any meal. It should be flavorful and refreshing and appealing to the eye. Part of its perfection will come from the skill with which you handle the greens, part from the care with which you cut up the other ingredients, and a third part comes from a good homemade dressing in proper amount.

If iceberg or Simpson lettuce is all you're accustomed to using for greens, break away and try others. They'll add new flavor and texture. The most interesting salads combine several greens. For instance:

Belgian endive	Escarole
Boston lettuce	Romaine
Celery cabbage	Young spinach
Chicory (curly endive)	Watercress

All greens enjoy the same treatment. Remove cores or ends and discard any damaged leaves. Place in a large amount of cold water to dislodge any soil. Remove from water and shake until nearly dry. Pat dry on paper towel.

To store greens, wrap them in paper towel and place in crisper of refrigerator.

Some of the vegetables you add to salad taste good if they are marinated for an hour or so in the dressing. Try any of the following:

Snipped fresh dill
Thin pennies of raw turnip
Thin slices of fresh mushroom
Thin sliced cauliflowerets

Other vegetables taste their best when they are combined with dressing just before serving:

Sliced celery	Sliced ripe or stuffed olives
Sliced radishes	Grated raw carrot
Sliced pared cucumbers	Thin tomato wedges
Diced green pepper	Thin sliced fennel (finocchio)

A tossed green salad may be assembled without the dressing, and chilled. At serving time each guest may add his own dressing. But better yet, select a dressing the whole family likes and toss it thoroughly with the vegetables so that every piece is coated.

Most people will eat about 1 cup of mixed green salad.

CHINESE SLAW

1 teaspoon Morton Lite Salt mixture
¼ teaspoon pepper
½ teaspoon dry mustard
2 tablespoons sugar
1 tablespoon grated onion

3 tablespoons vegetable oil
⅓ cup vinegar
5 cups (1¼ lbs.) diagonally cut Chinese celery cabbage

* * *

Watercress (optional)

In a salad bowl, mix all ingredients except cabbage. Add cabbage and toss to mix well. Cover and chill thoroughly. Serve garnished with watercress if desired. Makes 4 servings.

Per Serving

Calories	130	Sodium	297 mg.
Carbohydrate	9 Gm.	Potassium	684 mg.
Protein	trace	Cholesterol	0
Fat	11 Gm.		

GRAPEFRUIT AND MUSHROOM SALAD

½ cup grapefruit juice
¾ cup vegetable oil
½ teaspoon sugar
¼ teaspoon Morton Lite Salt mixture
⅛ teaspoon Tabasco
2 tablespoons chopped green onions

½ cup sliced fresh mushrooms
2 grapefruit, sectioned and chilled

* * *

Lettuce leaves
¼ cup sliced radishes

In medium bowl, beat together grapefruit juice, oil, sugar, salt and Tabasco. Stir in green onions and mushrooms. Cover and refrigerate for several hours. Divide and arrange grapefruit sections onto 4 plates lined with lettuce leaves. Pour grapefruit dressing over sections. Garnish with radish slices. Makes 4 servings.

Per Serving

Calories	163	Sodium	79 mg.
Carbohydrate	17 Gm.	Potassium	380 mg.
Protein	2 Gm.	Cholesterol	0
Fat	11 Gm.		

ITALIAN CARROT AND ZUCCHINI SALAD

2 large carrots, diagonally
sliced
1 cup water
1 teaspoon Morton Lite Salt
mixture
1 medium zucchini, sliced, or 2
cups
½ cup vegetable oil

¼ cup vinegar
¼ teaspoon pepper
¼ teaspoon tarragon
¼ teaspoon basil
⅛ to ¼ teaspoon oregano

* * *

Lettuce leaves

Cook carrots for 3 minutes in 1 cup of boiling water to
which you have added ¼ teaspoon of salt. Add zucchini;
cook 2 minutes, or until crisp-tender. Drain. Combine oil,
vinegar, remaining ¾ teaspoon of salt and seasonings.
Pour over hot vegetables. Cover and chill for several
hours. Drain, reserving dressing. Serve vegetables on crisp
lettuce leaves and pass the reserved dressing. Makes 4
servings.

Per Serving

Calories	266	Sodium	277 mg.
Carbohydrate	3 Gm.	Potassium	591 mg.
Protein	trace	Cholesterol	0
Fat	28 Gm.		

INVENT-YOUR-OWN JELLIED VEGETABLE
SALAD

1 envelope unflavored gelatin
½ cup cold water
¼ cup sugar
½ teaspoon Morton Lite Salt
mixture
2 to 4 tablespoons vinegar
1 tablespoon lemon juice

1 cup vegetable juice, bouillon
or homemade beef or
chicken broth
1½ cups finely shredded or
chopped raw or cooked vegetables or diced cooked meat

Sprinkle gelatin over cold water in a small saucepan to
soften. Place over low heat; stir constantly until gelatin
dissolves. Remove from heat. Add sugar, salt, vinegar,
lemon juice and other liquid and stir until sugar dissolves.
Pour into a bowl. Chill. When somewhat thickened and
very syrupy, fold in vegetables and/or meat, 1½ cups in

all. Pour into a 3-cup mold or bowl; chill until firm. Makes 4 servings.

GOOD ADDITIONS

Raw: Finely shredded red or green cabbage, spinach or carrot; chopped celery, green pepper, seeded cucumber or cauliflower; sliced green onions or radishes.

Cooked: Cut green beans, corn, asparagus, lima beans, sliced carrots, green peas, kidney beans, chick peas.

Meats and Seafoods: Diced cooked chicken, ham, tongue, pork or beef; flaked tuna.

Note: Do not add fresh pineapple or its juice to gelatin.

Per Serving (made with cocktail vegetable juice and mixture of carrots, corn and peas)

Calories	142	Sodium	318 mg.
Carbohydrate	25 Gm.	Potassium	175 mg.
Protein	12 Gm.	Cholesterol	0
Fat	trace		

TOMATO ASPIC

1 envelope unflavored gelatin
2 cups tomato juice
1 tablespoon lemon juice
½ teaspoon Morton Lite Salt mixture
1 teaspoon basil
2 teaspoons instant minced onions

¼ teaspoon instant minced garlic
⅛ teaspoon whole black pepper

* * *

Lettuce leaves

Sprinkle gelatin over ½ cup of the tomato juice to soften; set aside. In a small saucepan, combine 1½ cups of tomato juice with remaining ingredients. Bring to boil; reduce heat and simmer, uncovered, for 10 minutes. Strain into softened gelatin; stir until gelatin is dissolved. Pour into a 2-cup mold and chill for 3 hours, or until firm. Unmold and surround with crisp greens. Makes 4 servings.

Per Serving

Calories	47	Sodium	275 mg.
Carbohydrate	3 Gm.	Potassium	350 mg.
Protein	9 Gm.	Cholesterol	0
Fat	trace		

JELLIED GAZPACHO

1 envelope unflavored gelatin
½ cup water
1 cup homemade chicken broth
⅓ cup vinegar
1 teaspoon Morton Lite Salt mixture
1 teaspoon paprika
½ teaspoon basil
¼ teaspoon ground cloves

⅛ teaspoon Tabasco
1 clove garlic, minced
2 tablespoons minced onion
¼ cup minced celery
½ cup minced green pepper
1½ cups minced fresh tomato

* * *

Dairy sour cream, optional

Sprinkle gelatin on water in saucepan to soften. Place over low heat and stir until gelatin is dissolved. Remove from heat and add broth, vinegar, salt and seasonings. Mix well. Chill in refrigerator or bowl of ice water until it is the consistency of unbeaten egg white. Fold in minced vegetables. Cover and chill for at least 1 hour. Turn into soup bowls and garnish with sour cream. Makes 8 servings.

Per Serving

Calories	30	Sodium	156 mg.
Carbohydrate	3 Gm.	Potassium	156 mg.
Protein	5 Gm.	Cholesterol	1 mg.
Fat	trace		

PERFECTION SALAD

1 envelope unflavored gelatin
¼ cup sugar
½ teaspoon Morton Lite Salt mixture
1¼ cups water
¼ cup vinegar
1 tablespoon lemon juice
½ cup finely shredded cabbage

1 cup chopped celery
1 pimiento, cut in small pieces or 2 tablespoons chopped sweet red or green pepper

* * *

Crisp greens
Mayonnaise-type dressing

Mix gelatin, sugar and salt well in small saucepan. Add ½ cup of the water. Place over low heat, stirring constantly until gelatin is dissolved. Remove from heat, stir in remaining ¾ cup of water, vinegar and lemon juice. Chill until thick and syrupy. Fold in vegetables. Turn into a 2-cup mold or individual molds and chill until firm. Unmold: garnish with greens. Serve with mayonnaise-type dressing. Makes 4 servings.

Per Serving

Calories	94	Sodium	183 mg.
Carbohydrate	16 Gm.	Potassium	225 mg.
Protein	9 Gm.	Cholesterol	0
Fat	trace		

MACARONI SALAD, ITALIAN STYLE

8 ozs. elbow macaroni
3 quarts water
2 tablespoons Morton Lite Salt mixture
1 small onion, minced
¼ cup chopped parsley
1 green pepper, minced
1 pimiento, minced
¼ teaspoon pepper
½ teaspoon dry mustard
2 tablespoons vinegar or lemon juice
⅓ cup vegetable oil

Add macaroni gradually to 3 quarts of rapidly boiling water to which you have added 4 teaspoons of salt. Cook for 8 to 10 minutes, or until barely tender. Drain in colander and rinse with cold water. Add onion, parsley, green pepper and pimiento. Mix 2 teaspoons of salt with remaining ingredients; toss gently with macaroni mixture to blend well. Chill. Makes 6 servings.

Per Serving

Calories	174	Sodium	1109 mg.
Carbohydrate	10 Gm.	Potassium	833 mg.
Protein	2 Gm.	Cholesterol	0
Fat	14 Gm.		

OLD-FASHIONED MACARONI SALAD

8 ozs. elbow macaroni
3 quarts water
5 teaspoons Morton Lite Salt mixture
½ cup mayonnaise
1 tablespoon lemon juice
1 teaspoon sugar
¼ teaspoon celery seed

1 tomato, diced
1 cup diced celery
3 tablespoons chopped pimien-to
2 tablespoons chopped green pepper

* * *

Salad greens

Add macaroni gradually to 3 quarts of rapidly boiling water to which you have added 4 teaspoons salt. Cook for 8 to 10 minutes, or until barely tender. Drain, rinse with cold water, drain again. Mix mayonnaise with lemon juice, 1 teaspoon of salt and 1 teaspoon sugar. Combine with macaroni, celery seed, tomato, celery, pimiento and green pepper. Chill thoroughly. To serve, garnish with salad greens. Makes 8 servings.

Per Serving

Calories	216	Sodium	324 mg.
Carbohydrate	10 Gm.	Potassium	316 mg.
Protein	2 Gm.	Cholesterol	20 mg.
Fat	18 Gm.		

POTATO SALAD FOR A CROWD

5 lbs. potatoes
2 tablespoons Morton Lite Salt mixture
2 eggs
¼ cup lemon juice
¼ cup vinegar
¼ teaspoon pepper
⅔ cup minced sweet onion
⅔ cup minced green pepper

½ cup minced parsley
2 cups diced celery
½ cup grated carrot
2 cups whipped salad dressing or mayonnaise
⅓ cup prepared mustard
1 tablespoon sugar
Paprika

Scrub potatoes well and remove eyes. Leave small potatoes whole, halve larger ones. Put in large saucepan with water to cover and 1 tablespoon of the salt. Rest unshelled raw eggs on potatoes. Cover and boil gently for 10 minutes. With slotted spoon, remove eggs and place in cold water. Cook potatoes for 5 to 10 minutes more. Test frequently—they should be barely tender. Drain. Meantime, in a large mixing bowl, measure out lemon juice, vinegar, pepper, the remaining tablespoon of salt and sweet onion. Mix and allow to coat sides of bowl. Peel and slice potatoes while still hot. Place in bowl, tossing mixture from time to time. Let cool about 15 minutes. Add green pepper, parsley, celery and carrot; toss gently. Chop eggs and mix with mayonnaise, mustard and sugar. Toss with potato mixture. Place in serving bowl, cover and chill at least 2 hours. Just before serving, garnish with paprika. Makes 12 to 15 servings.

Per Serving

Calories	409	Sodium	508 mg.
Carbohydrate	37 Gm.	Potassium	1033 mg.
Protein	6 Gm.	Cholesterol	72 mg.
Fat	26 Gm.		

FRUIT SALADS

Fruit salads perk up many menus. They add sweetness and sometimes tartness, and always lend a touch of color. Some hostesses do not put their fruit salad on lettuce, but leave it in a bowl and serve it with a pierced spoon into small dishes. Some guests enjoy it with the meal; for others it suffices as dessert.

Dressings are not strictly necessary for fruit salads, but they add piquancy and zest and help marry the flavor of the salad to the meat you are serving. Many sweet fruit dressings are offered here, but classic French dressing and mayonnaise are also good toppers.

The green base for most fruit salads may be Simpson or iceberg lettuce, as leaves or shredded, or cups of soft Boston lettuce. Watercress is also good, especially in combination with orange or grapefruit sections.

It's nice to use fresh fruits when they are in season,

alone or in combination. Canned fruits, though higher in calories, are flavorful and colorful.

Mix-match salads by selecting from the following list of fruits and toppings:

Apples,* preferably unpeeled, chopped, or in crescents
Apricots, fresh halved or diced or stewed halves
Avocados,* diced or in crescents or rings
Bananas,* sliced or cut in half
Berries of all kinds
Cantaloupes in chunks, crescents or balls
Cherries, pitted
Grapefruit, sections or half sections
Grapes, Thompson seedless or pitted red or purple
Honeydew, in crescents or balls
Papaya in chunks or crescents
Nectarines,* halved or sliced
Oranges, sliced, sectioned or diced
Peaches,* halved and pitted, crescents or diced
Pears,* halved and pitted, crescents or diced
Pineapple rings, chunks or tidbits

Plums, peeled and halved or diced
Prunes, whole pitted or halved
Tangerines (Mandarin oranges), sections

Toppers: Cottage cheese, cream cheese, chopped walnuts or slivered pecans, Brazil nuts or almonds, whole almonds or peanuts, maraschino cherries, lime or lemon slices or wedges, paprika.

*These fruits are likely to darken on standing. To prevent this, dip fruit in lemon, orange or pineapple juice.

PINK GRAPEFRUIT SALAD

2 grapefruit, peeled and sectioned
¼ cup sliced water chestnuts
½ teaspoon Morton Lite Salt mixture

⅓ cup grenadine syrup
Lettuce leaves

* * *

Avocado Dressing (page 144)

Arrange the well-trimmed grapefruit sections over the bottom of a shallow casserole or deep platter. Spread water chestnut slices over top. Sprinkle with salt. Pour grenadine syrup over all. Refrigerate, covered, for 4 hours. Place lettuce on each of 4 salad plates. Portion fruit onto plates. Garnish with Avocado Dressing and pass the remainder of the dressing at the table. Makes 4 servings.

Per Serving (without dressing)

Calories	42	Sodium	144 mg.
Carbohydrate	10 Gm.	Potassium	300 mg.
Protein	1 Gm.	Cholesterol	0
Fat	trace		

INVENT-YOUR-OWN JELLIED FRUIT SALAD

1 envelope unflavored gelatin
½ cup cold water
¼ cup sugar
½ teaspoon Morton Lite Salt mixture
2 tablespoons vinegar

1 tablespoon lemon juice
1 cup fresh, frozen or canned fruit juice*
1½ cups fresh, frozen or canned fruits*

Sprinkle gelatin over cold water in a small saucepan to soften. Place over low heat; stir constantly until gelatin dissolves (no granules visible), about 3 minutes. Remove from heat. Add sugar, salt, vinegar, lemon juice and fruit juice, and stir until sugar dissolves. Pour into a bowl. Chill. When somewhat thickened and very syrupy, fold in fruit: chill until firm. Makes 4 servings.

For fruit juice: Besides fresh, frozen and canned juices, you may use fruit punches, nectars and fruit ades.

For fruits: Fresh, frozen or canned peaches, plums, pears, apricots, berries of all varieties, melons, bananas, grapes, cherries, canned pineapple and fruit cocktail.

Per Serving (made with orange juice and fruit cocktail)

Calories	169	Sodium	154 mg.
Carbohydrate	34 Gm.	Potassium	200 mg.
Protein	9 Gm.	Cholesterol	0
Fat	trace		

*Fresh pineapple contains an enzyme which resists jelling, so do not use it, or fresh pineapple juice, unless you boil it for 2 minutes before adding to dissolved gelatin.

PINEAPPLE RELISH MOLD

2 envelopes unflavored gelatin
½ cup cold water
1 can (1 lb. 4½ oz.) crushed pineapple in syrup
2 tablespoons sugar
½ teaspoon Morton Lite Salt mixture

¼ cup vinegar
3 tablespoons lemon juice
1 cup chopped celery
½ cup chopped green pepper
2 pimientos, minced

* * *

Crisp greens

Sprinkle gelatin over cold water in medium saucepan. Drain syrup from pineapple into 2-cup measure; add enough water to the syrup to make 2 cups and then add ½ cup of this mixture to gelatin in saucepan. Place saucepan over low heat; stir constantly until gelatin dissolves (about 5 minutes). Remove from heat; stir in sugar, salt, remaining syrup mixture, vinegar and lemon juice. Chill, stirring occasionally, until mixture mounds slightly when dropped from spoon. Fold in drained crushed pineapple, celery, green pepper and pimientos. Turn into 4-cup mold. Chill until firm. Unmold onto serving platter and garnish with greens. Makes 6 servings.

Per Serving

Calories	102	Sodium	132 mg.
Carbohydrate	15 Gm.	Potassium	300 mg.
Protein	12 Gm.	Cholesterol	0
Fat	trace		

JELLIED WALDORF SALAD

1 envelope unflavored gelatin
1½ cups cold water
⅓ cup sugar
¼ teaspoon Morton Lite Salt mixture
¼ cup lemon juice

2 cups diced unpared tart apple
½ cup chopped celery
¼ cup chopped pecans

* * *

Salad greens

Sprinkle gelatin over ½ cup of the cold water in saucepan to soften. Place over low heat; stir constantly until gelatin dissolves (about 5 minutes). Remove from heat; stir in sugar, salt, remaining 1 cup of water and lemon juice. Chill, stirring occasionally, until it is the consistency of unbeaten egg white. Fold in apple, celery and pecans. Turn into a 4-cup mold. Chill until firm. Unmold and garnish with salad greens. Makes 6 servings.

Per Serving

Calories	145	Sodium	65 mg.
Carbohydrate	25 Gm.	Potassium	116 mg.
Protein	7 Gm.	Cholesterol	0
Fat	3 Gm.		

BASIC FRENCH DRESSING

1 cup vegetable oil
⅓ to ½ cup vinegar (substitute some lemon juice if desired)
1 to 3 tablespoons sugar

1½ teaspoons Morton Lite Salt mixture
½ teaspoon paprika
½ teaspoon dry mustard
1 clove garlic, halved

Measure all ingredients into bottle or jar. Cover tightly and shake well. Chill several hours, then remove garlic. Shake well before serving. Makes 1⅓ to 1½ cups.

Per Recipe

Calories	2174	Sodium	1685 mg.
Carbohydrate	43 Gm.	Potassium	2200 mg.
Protein	trace	Cholesterol	0
Fat	224 Gm.		

TRUE ITALIAN DRESSING

⅔ cup vegetable oil
3 tablespoons white vinegar
1 tablespoon water
2 teaspoons Morton Lite Salt mixture

1 teaspoon sugar
1½ teaspoons lemon juice
¼ teaspoon garlic powder
Dash red pepper
Dash crushed oregano

Measure all ingredients into bottle or jar. Cover tightly and shake well. Chill at least 1 hour. Shake well before serving. Makes about 1 cup.

Per Recipe

Calories	787	Sodium	2202 mg.
Carbohydrate	9 Gm.	Potassium	3000 mg.
Protein	0	Cholesterol	0
Fat	84 Gm.		

,TOMATO SALAD DRESSING

¾ cup chilled tomato juice
2 tablespoons lemon juice
2 tablespoons instant minced onion
1 tablespoon basil

½ teaspoon Morton Lite Salt mixture
¼ teaspoon garlic powder
⅛ teaspoon ground cumin seed
⅛ teaspoon ground red pepper

In a small jar, combine all ingredients and blend well. Makes 1 cup.

Per Recipe

Calories	392	Sodium	1005 mg.
Carbohydrate	92 Gm.	Potassium	1533 mg.
Protein	10 Gm.	Cholesterol	0
Fat	1 Gm.		

MORTON LITE SALT MAYONNAISE

1 cup vegetable oil
1 egg
2 tablespoons wine vinegar
1 teaspoon sugar

1 teaspoon dry mustard
¾ teaspoon Morton Lite Salt mixture
Dash cayenne pepper

In an electric blender jar, measure ¼ cup of the oil, plus all remaining ingredients. Cover and blend on high speed for 2 seconds, or until thoroughly mixed. Remove cover and turn speed to low. *Very slowly,* in thinnest possible stream, add additional oil while blender agitates. If a pool of oil forms in the center of the blending mixture, stop blender and agitate contents a little with a rubber spatula. Continue blending and adding the remaining oil until well mixed. Store covered in refrigerator. Makes one generous cup.

Per Recipe

Calories	2128	Sodium	956 mg.
Carbohydrate	6 Gm.	Potassium	1088 mg.
Protein	7 Gm.	Cholesterol	272 mg.
Fat	231 Gm.		

COOKED SALAD DRESSING

2 teaspoons cornstarch	1 teaspoon Morton Lite Salt
1 teaspoon dry mustard	mixture
¼ teaspoon paprika	¼ cup unsalted polyunsatu-
⅛ teaspoon white pepper	rated margarine
1 cup milk	2 tablespoons vinegar

In saucepan, combine cornstarch, mustard, paprika and pepper. Slowly stir in milk. Bring to a boil, stirring constantly; boil 2 minutes. Add salt and margarine. Cook 2 minutes longer. Remove from heat. With rotary beater, beat in vinegar. Cool. Before serving, beat until creamy. Makes about 1¼ cups.

Per Recipe

Calories	627	Sodium	1228 mg.
Carbohydrate	21 Gm.	Potassium	1816 mg.
Protein	9 Gm.	Cholesterol	26 mg.
Fat	58 Gm.		

SWEET MAYONNAISE DRESSING

⅔ cup sugar
2 teaspoons dry mustard
3 tablespoons cornstarch
1 teaspoon Morton Lite Salt
  mixture

2 eggs
½ cup vinegar
½ cup water
1 pint mayonnaise

In a saucepan, combine sugar, mustard, cornstarch and salt. Beat in eggs, one at a time. Mix vinegar and water and beat in gradually. Cook over moderate heat, beating from time to time, until mixture begins to boil, loses its foam and becomes compact and shiny. Cool for 15 minutes. Fold in mayonnaise. Keep refrigerated. Makes about 3 cups.

Per Recipe

Calories	3582	Sodium	4036 mg.
Carbohydrate	178 Gm.	Potassium	1680 mg.
Protein	15 Gm.	Cholesterol	864 mg.
Fat	301 Gm.		

EASY LEMON DRESSING

1 cup vegetable oil

4 teaspoons sugar
½ cup lemon juice

Combine all ingredients. Keep refrigerated.

Per Recipe

Calories	2110	Sodium	1 mg.
Carbohydrate	26 Gm.	Potassium	1 mg.
Protein	1 Gm.	Cholesterol	0
Fat	224 Gm.		

CITRUS HONEY DRESSING

½ cup vegetable oil
2 tablespoons grapefruit juice
2 tablespoons orange juice
2 tablespoons lemon juice
¼ cup honey

2 teaspoons Morton Lite Salt mixture
½ teaspoon paprika
Dash cayenne

Combine all ingredients in a small jar and shake until thoroughly blended. Makes about 1 cup.

Per Recipe

Calories	1327	Sodium	2208 mg.
Carbohydrate	81 Gm.	Potassium	3150 mg.
Protein	1 Gm.	Cholesterol	0
Fat	112 Gm.		

ORANGE POPPYSEED DRESSING

⅔ cup vegetable oil
¼ cup red wine vinegar
½ teaspoon Morton Lite Salt mixture

1 tablespoon poppyseed
2 teaspoons grated orange peel

Combine all ingredients in jar. Seal and shake vigorously. Chill 2 hours to develop flavor. Makes 1 cup.

Per Recipe

Calories	1267	Sodium	551 mg.
Carbohydrate	3 Gm.	Potassium	760 mg.
Protein	0	Cholesterol	0
Fat	140 Gm.		

PINK POPPYSEED DRESSING

½ cup sugar
1 teaspoon Morton Lite Salt mixture
1 teaspoon dry mustard
½ teaspoon grated lemon peel
2 teaspoons minced onion

⅓ cup lemon juice
¾ cup vegetable oil
Few drops red food coloring, if desired
1 tablespoon poppyseeds

Measure all ingredients except food color and poppyseeds into jar of electric blender. Cover and blend until well mixed. If desired, add food color, drop by drop, to tint a delicate pink. Stir in poppyseeds. Keep refrigerated. Makes 1½ cups.

Per Recipe

Calories	936	Sodium	1207 mg.
Carbohydrate	211 Gm.	Potassium	1600 mg.
Protein	13 Gm.	Cholesterol	0
Fat	14 Gm.		

AVOCADO DRESSING

1 medium avocado, pitted and peeled
¼ cup mayonnaise
4 to 5 teaspoons lemon juice

½ teaspoon Morton Lite Salt mixture
2 to 4 drops Tabasco

In small bowl of electric mixer, combine all ingredients. Blend at low speed, then beat at medium speed for 2 to 3 minutes, or until fluffy. (Dressing will be slightly lumpy.) Or measure into jar of electric blender and blend until smooth. Enough for 4 servings.

Per Recipe

Calories	513	Sodium	888 mg.
Carbohydrate	8 Gm.	Potassium	1120 mg.
Protein	2 Gm.	Cholesterol	40 mg.
Fat	52 Gm.		

CHAPTER 7

BREADS, PLAIN AND SWEET

CHAPTER 7

BREADS, PLAIN AND SWEET

Homemade bread is so much fun to make and so wholesome in flavor, texture and appearance that you should make it often. Plus, when you make your own bread, you can be sure of exactly what ingredients are included. And you'll have had the personal bonus of an afternoon spent with the fragrance of yeast, that perfume which makes bakeries such attractive places.

The breads which follow use modern mixing techniques so they'll take less time and effort than Grandma's favorite "receipts."

Toward the end of the chapter you'll find sweet yeast breads. These recipes are very useful since they contain no baking powder or baking soda and are good, too!

Some quick breads are also included: puffy popovers, biscuits low in saturated fat and appetizing Sesame Twists.

You'll enjoy making breads from scratch, and your baking is sure to win enthusiastic compliments from family and friends.

GOOD WHITE BREAD

About 7 cups flour
3 tablespoons sugar
2 teaspoons Morton Lite Salt mixture
1 package active dry yeast

1½ cups water
½ cup milk
3 tablespoons unsalted polyunsaturated margarine

In large bowl of electric mixer, thoroughly mix 2 cups of the flour with the sugar, salt and undissolved yeast. Combine water, milk and margarine in a saucepan. Heat over low heat until liquids are warm to the touch (120 to 130°). (Margarine need not melt.) Gradually add liquids to dry ingredients and beat 2 minutes at medium speed of electric mixer, scraping bowl occasionally. Add enough more flour (about ¾ cup) to make a thick batter and beat at high speed for 2 minutes, scraping the bowl occasionally. Stir in enough of remaining flour to make a soft dough. Turn out onto a lightly floured board and knead until smooth and elastic (about 8 to 10 minutes). (To knead, push dough with palms of hands against cupped fingers; twist one-quarter turn; repeat.) Place in a greased bowl, turning so top is also oiled. Cover; let rise in a warm place (80 to 85°), free from draft, until doubled in bulk (1 hour).

Punch dough down; turn out onto lightly floured board. Cover and let rest for 15 minutes. Divide dough in half and mold into loaves. Place in 2 greased loaf pans, 8½″ × 4½″ × 2½″. Cover; let rise in warm place, free from draft until doubled in bulk (1 hour). Bake at 400° for 25 to 30 minutes, or until done. (Test by tipping loaf out of pan and tapping bottom; there should be a hollow sound.) Remove from pans and cool on wire racks before slicing. Makes 2 loaves.

Per Slice

Calories	107	Sodium	73 mg.
Carbohydrate	21 Gm.	Potassium	103 mg.
Protein	4 Gm.	Cholesterol	trace
Fat	trace		

ONION BREAD ROUNDS

1 cup warm—not hot—water	2½ to 3 cups unsifted flour
1 package active dry yeast	¼ cup unsalted polyunsaturated
2 teaspoons sugar	margarine, melted
1½ teaspoons Morton Lite	¾ cup chopped onion
Salt mixture	

Measure warm water into a warmed mixing bowl. Sprinkle in yeast; stir until dissolved. Add sugar, 1 teaspoon of the salt and 2 cups of the flour. Beat vigorously until well blended. Add enough of remaining flour to make a stiff dough. Turn out onto lightly floured board and knead until smooth and elastic (about 5 minutes). Place in a greased bowl, turning to grease top. Cover; let rise in warm place, free from draft, until doubled in bulk (about 1 hour).

Punch dough down; divide in half. Cover and let rest for 5 minutes. Pat dough into 2 greased 9-inch-round cake pans. Brush tops with melted margarine and sprinkle with onion. Press onions into dough with fingertips until entire surface looks dented. Let rise, covered, in a warm place free from draft until doubled in bulk (about 45 minutes). Sprinkle tops with remaining ½ teaspoon of salt. Bake at 450° for 20 to 25 minutes, or until firm and hollow-sounding when tapped on top. Cool in pans on wire racks. Best when served warm. Makes two 9-inch rounds.

Per Serving (⅛ round)

Calories	123	Sodium	108 mg.
Carbohydrate	19 Gm.	Potassium	206 mg.
Protein	5 Gm.	Cholesterol	0
Fat	3 Gm.		

ONE-BOWL LOW-FAT BREAD

7 to 8 cups unsifted flour
2 tablespoons sugar
2 teaspoons Morton Lite Salt mixture

1 package active dry yeast
1 tablespoon unsalted polyunsaturated margarine, softened
2½ cups very hot water

In the large bowl of the electric mixer, thoroughly mix 2½ cups of the flour, sugar, salt and undissolved yeast. Add soft margarine. Gradually add very hot tap water to dry ingredients and beat 2 minutes at medium speed of electric mixer, scraping bowl occasionally. Add ¾ cup of flour, or enough to make a thick batter; beat at high speed for 2 minutes, scraping bowl occasionally. Stir in enough of remaining flour to make a soft dough. Turn out onto lightly floured board; knead until smooth and elastic (about 8 to 10 minutes). Place in a greased bowl, turning to grease top. Cover; let rise in a warm place, free from draft, until doubled in bulk (about 1 hour).

Punch dough down; turn out onto lightly floured board. Divide dough in half; shape each half into a loaf. Place in 2 greased loaf pans 9″ × 5″ × 3″. Cover; let rise in warm place, free from draft, until doubled in bulk (about 1 hour).

Bake at 400° for about 30 to 35 minutes, or until loaf sounds hollow when tipped out of pan and tapped on bottom. Remove from pans and cool on wire racks before slicing. Makes 2 loaves.

Per Slice

Calories	112	Sodium	71 mg.
Carbohydrate	23 Gm.	Potassium	96 mg.
Protein	4 Gm.	Cholesterol	0
Fat	trace		

ALL WHOLE WHEAT BREAD

8¾ to 9¾ cups unsifted whole wheat flour
4 teaspoons Morton Lite Salt mixture
2 packages active dry yeast
1½ cups milk
1½ cups water
½ cup honey
6 tablespoons unsalted polyunsaturated margarine

In large bowl of electric mixer, thoroughly mix 3 cups of the flour with salt and undissolved yeast. Combine milk, water, honey and margarine in a saucepan. Heat over low heat until liquids are warm (120 to 130°). (Margarine does not need to melt.) Gradually add to dry ingredients and beat 2 minutes at medium speed, scraping bowl occasionally. Add 1 cup of the flour, or enough to make a thick batter. Beat at high speed for 2 minutes, scraping bowl occasionally. Stir in enough of remaining flour to make a soft dough. Turn out onto lightly floured board; cover dough with bowl and let rest for 10 minutes. Then remove bowl and knead until smooth and elastic (about 8 to 10 minutes). Place in greased bowl, turning to grease top. Cover; let rise in warm place, free from draft, until doubled in bulk (about 1 hour).

Punch dough down; turn out onto lightly floured board. Divide in half. Shape each half into a loaf. Place in 2 greased 9″ × 5″ × 3″ loaf pans. Cover; let rise in warm place, free from draft, until doubled in bulk (about 1 hour).

Bake at 375° for 35 to 40 minutes, or until loaf sounds hollow when tipped out of pan and tapped on bottom. Remove from pans and cool on wire rack. Makes 2 loaves.

Per Slice

Calories	183	Sodium	148 mg.
Carbohydrate	33 Gm.	Potassium	184 mg.
Protein	8 Gm.	Cholesterol	1 mg.
Fat	4 Gm.		

POPPYSEED BATTER BREAD

1¼ cups warm—not hot—
  water*
1 package active dry yeast
2 tablespoons unsalted polyunsaturated margarine
2 tablespoons poppyseeds
2 tablespoons sugar

2 teaspoons Morton Lite Salt
  mixture
3 to 3½ cups unsifted flour
1 egg white
1 tablespoon cold water
Additional poppyseeds

Measure warm water into large warm bowl. Sprinkle in yeast; stir until dissolved. Add margarine, 2 tablespoons of poppyseeds, sugar and salt. Stir in 2 cups of flour. Beat until well blended (about 1 minute). Stir in enough of remaining flour to make a soft dough. Cover; let rise in warm place, free from draft, until doubled in bulk (about 35 minutes).

Stir down. Spread evenly in greased loaf pan, 9″ × 5″ × 3″. Cover; let rise in warm place, free from draft, until doubled in bulk (about 40 minutes).

Combine egg white and cold water; carefully brush onto top of loaf. Sprinkle with poppyseeds. Bake at 375° for about 45 minutes, or until loaf sounds hollow when tipped out of pan and tapped on bottom. Remove from pan and cool on wire rack. Makes 1 loaf.

Per Slice

Calories	125	Sodium	144 mg.
Carbohydrate	22 Gm.	Potassium	193 mg.
Protein	5 Gm.	Cholesterol	0
Fat	2 Gm.		

*110°

POPOVERS

½ cup milk
1 tablespoon melted unsalted polyunsaturated margarine
1 egg

½ cup flour
¼ teaspoon Morton Lite Salt mixture

In medium mixing bowl, combine ingredients in order given. Beat with rotary beater just until smooth. Fill well-greased 5-oz. custard cups half full of batter. Bake at 425° for 15 minutes, then reduce heat to 350° and bake 15 minutes longer. Remove from custard cups at once and make small slit in side of each popover to allow steam to escape. Serve hot. Makes 6.

Note: Popover or muffin pans may also be used, filling the greased pans half full. Yield will vary with size of pans.

Per Serving

Calories	78	Sodium	67 mg.
Carbohydrate	8 Gm.	Potassium	70 mg.
Protein	3 Gm.	Cholesterol	43 mg.
Fat	4 Gm.		

FLAKY BISCUITS

2 cups sifted flour
3 teaspoons baking powder
1 teaspoon Morton Lite Salt mixture

⅓ cup vegetable oil
⅔ cup milk

Sift flour, baking powder and salt together into a bowl. Blend in vegetable oil with fork or pastry blender. Add milk; mix until dough forms. Gently knead on a lightly floured board 15 to 20 times. Roll or pat out to half-inch thickness. Cut with floured biscuit cutter. Place onto ungreased cookie sheet. Bake at 450° for 12 to 15 minutes, or until lightly browned. Makes twelve 2-inch biscuits.

Per Serving

Calories	103	Sodium	95 mg.
Carbohydrate	14 Gm.	Potassium	83 mg.
Protein	2 Gm.	Cholesterol	trace
Fat	4 Gm.		

SESAME TWISTS

¼ cup sesame seeds
1 cup flour
¼ cup shortening
¾ teaspoon Morton Lite Salt
  mixture

2 to 4 tablespoons water
3 tablespoons unsalted polyunsaturated margarine, softened
½ teaspoon paprika
2 to 4 drops Tabasco

Place sesame seeds in small skillet over medium heat; stir constantly until toasted golden brown. Remove from skillet and let cool. In medium mixing bowl, combine flour, shortening and ½ teaspoon of the salt. With pastry blender, cut in shortening until crumbly. Add water, using the least amount possible, and stir with fork until dough forms a ball. Roll out onto floured surface to form a rectangle 10 by 14 inches.

Combine toasted sesame seeds with margarine, paprika, remaining ¼ teaspoon of salt and Tabasco to taste. With back of spoon, blend until well mixed. Spread this mixture down one lengthwise half of pastry. Fold plain side over top to form a rectangle 5 by 14 inches. Trim edges to make them even. Cut the folded pastry into half inch strips. Twist each pastry to make 4 turns. Place onto ungreased 15″ × 17″ baking sheet, ½ inch apart. To maintain twist, press each end down gently but firmly. Bake at 400° for 12 to 18 minutes, or until golden. Serve hot. Makes about 20.

Note: After cooling, twists may be frozen; use within 2 weeks.

Per Serving

Calories	66	Sodium	538 mg.
Carbohydrate	8 Gm.	Potassium	70 mg.
Protein	3 Gm.	Cholesterol	8 mg.
Fat	trace		

1 package active dry yeast
¼ cup warm—not hot—water*
¾ cup milk, scalded and cooled to lukewarm
¼ cup sugar

1 teaspoon Morton Lite Salt mixture
1 egg
¼ cup unsalted polyunsaturated margarine, softened
3½ to 3¾ cups flour

In large bowl, dissolve yeast in warm water. Add milk, sugar, salt, egg, margarine and half of the flour. Mix with spoon until smooth. Add enough remaining flour to handle easily; mix with hand or spoon. Turn onto lightly floured board; knead until smooth and elastic (about 5 minutes). Place in large greased mixing bowl; turn dough over so top side is greased. Cover; let rise in warm place (85°) until double, about 1½ hours. Punch down; let rise again until almost double (about ½ hour). Shape into Cinnamon Rolls or Swedish Tea Ring. Bake as directed.

Per 2 Cinnamon Rolls

Calories	306	Sodium	163 mg.
Carbohydrate	47 Gm.	Potassium	312 mg.
Protein	11 Gm.	Cholesterol	41 mg.
Fat	8 Gm.		

* 110°

CINNAMON ROLLS

Roll dough into an oblong 15″ × 9″. Spread with 2 tablespoons of softened margarine and sprinkle with a mixture of ½ cup of sugar and 2 teaspoons of cinnamon. Roll up tightly, beginning at wide side. Pinch edges of roll together. Cut into 1-inch slices. Place in greased pan, 13″ × 9″ × 2″, or 18 greased muffin cups. Cover; let rise until doubled (35 to 40 minutes). Bake at 375° 25 to 30 minutes. Frost with mixture of 1 cup of confectioners' sugar, 1 tablespoon of water, milk or cream, and ½ teaspoon of vanilla. Makes about 18 rolls.

SWEDISH TEA RING

Begin by following the recipe for Cinnamon Rolls, sprinkling dough with ½ cup of raisins in addition to sugar. Roll up dough as for above, but do not cut into slices. Instead, shape dough into a ring on a greased baking sheet, seam side down. Pinch ends together. With scissors, cut ⅔ of the way through the ring at 1-inch intervals. Turn each 1-inch section on its side. Let rise until doubled (35 to 40 minutes). Bake at 375° for 25 to 30 minutes. Frost while warm with confectioners' sugar mixture in Cinnamon Roll recipe. If desired, decorate with nuts and cherries. Makes 1 tea ring.

OLD-FASHIONED DOUGHNUTS WITH A BONUS

1 cup warm—not hot—water*
2 packages active dry yeast
⅔ cup sugar
1 teaspoon Morton Lite Salt mixture
½ cup mashed potatoes at room temperature
6 tablespoons soft unsalted polyunsaturated margarine

1 egg, at room temperature
4 to 5 cups unsifted flour
¼ cup light brown sugar
2 tablespoons light corn syrup
18 pecan halves
Vegetable oil for frying

Measure water into large warm bowl. Sprinkle in yeast; stir until dissolved. Stir in sugar, salt, potatoes and ¼ cup of the margarine. Add the egg and 2 cups of the flour; beat until smooth. Stir in enough additional flour to make a soft dough. Turn out onto lightly floured board; knead until smooth and elastic (8 to 10 minutes). Place in a greased bowl, turning to grease top. Cover; let rise in a warm place, free from draft, until doubled in bulk (about 1 hour). While dough rises, in a saucepan mix brown sugar, corn syrup and remaining 2 tablespoons of margarine. Heat, stirring, until margarine melts. Divide evenly among six greased muffin pans, 2½-inch cup size. Arrange 3 pecan halves in bottom of each cup. Set aside.

* 110°

Punch dough down; turn onto lightly floured board. Roll dough out ½ inch thick. Cut with 2½-inch doughnut cutter. Place on greased baking sheets.

Arrange 5 doughnut "holes" in each muffin cup to form "bonus" Pecan Rolls. Reroll dough as needed to complete cutting. Cover; let rise in warm place, free from draft, until doubled (about 1 hour).

Heat oil to 375°. Add doughnuts, 2 or 3 at a time, and fry one minute on each side. Drain on paper toweling. If desired, shake in bag with confectioners' sugar or mixture of granulated sugar and cinnamon.

Meantime, bake Pecan Rolls at 350° for about 20 minutes, or until firm and browned. Immediately invert rolls onto platter to cool.

Makes 30 doughnuts and 6 Pecan Rolls.

Per Serving

Calories	149	Sodium	48 mg.
Carbohydrate	26 Gm.	Potassium	63 mg.
Protein	4 Gm.	Cholesterol	trace
Fat	4 Gm.		

OATMEAL BATTER BREAD

¾ cup boiling water
½ cup rolled oats
3 tablespoons unsalted polyunsaturated margarine
¼ cup light molasses
2 teaspoons Morton Lite Salt
mixture

1 package active dry yeast
¼ cup warm—not hot—
water*
1 egg
2¾ cups flour

In large bowl of electric mixer, stir together boiling water, oats, margarine, molasses and salt. Cool to lukewarm. Dissolve yeast in warm water. Add it, along with egg and half the flour, to the lukewarm oat mixture. Beat for 2 minutes at medium speed of electric mixer, or 300 vigorous strokes by hand. Scrape sides and bottom of bowl frequently. Add the remaining flour and mix with a spoon until flour is blended in. Spread batter evenly in greased loaf pan, 8½″ × 4½″ × 2¾″ or 9″ × 5″ × 3″. Batter will be sticky. With floured hand, smooth out top of loaf. Let rise in warm place (85°) until batter reaches top of 8½-inch pan or 1 inch from top of 9-inch pan (about 1½ hours). Bake at 375° for 50 to 55 minutes. To test loaf, tap top crust; it should have a hollow sound. Crust will be dark brown. Immediately remove from pan. If desired, brush top with additional melted margarine. Cool before slicing. Makes 1 loaf (16 slices).

Orange Oatmeal Bread: Add ¼ cup of finely grated orange peel with first addition of flour.

Per Slice

Calories	128	Sodium	149 mg.
Carbohydrate	22 Gm.	Potassium	194 mg.
Protein	5 Gm.	Cholesterol	17 mg.
Fat	2 Gm.		

*110°

STREUSEL COFFEE CAKE

1 cup warm—not hot—water*
2 packages active dry yeast
½ teaspoon Morton Lite
  Salt mixture
4 cups (about) unsifted flour

½ cup unsalted polyunsaturated margarine
½ cup sugar
2 eggs

* * *

Streusel Topping

Measure warm water into warm mixing bowl. Sprinkle in yeast and stir until dissolved. Stir in salt and 1½ cups of the flour; beat until smooth. Cover; let rise in a warm place, free from draft, until doubled in bulk (about 30 minutes). Beat margarine until fluffy. Add sugar and beat until well mixed. Now add margarine mixture, eggs, and enough additional flour to make a soft dough into the rising "sponge." Turn out onto lightly floured board. Knead until smooth and elastic (about 5 minutes). Place in a greased bowl, turning to grease top. Cover; let rise in warm place, free from draft, until doubled in bulk (about 1 hour).

Divide dough into thirds. Press into 3 greased 8-inch cake pans. Cover; let rise until doubled in bulk (about 30 minutes). Sprinkle with Streusel Topping. Bake at 400° for about 20 minutes, or until firm and well browned. Makes three 8-inch cakes.

Streusel Topping: Beat ⅓ cup of unsalted polyunsaturated margarine until fluffy. Add ⅓ cup of sugar gradually, then stir in 1 cup of unsifted flour and 1 teaspoon of cinnamon. Mixture will be crumbly.

1/24th Recipe

Calories	149	Sodium	33 mg.
Carbohydrate	28 Gm.	Potassium	47 mg.
Protein	6 Gm.	Cholesterol	23 mg.
Fat	2 Gm.		

*110°

160

3½ to 4½ cups unsifted flour
½ cup sugar
1 teaspoon Morton Lite Salt
  mixture
1 package active dry yeast
1 cup milk
¼ cup water
½ cup unsalted polyunsaturated margarine

1 egg at room temperature
Filling:
½ cup unsifted flour
½ cup chopped pecans
½ cup light brown sugar
1 can (1 lb.) pitted red sour
  cherries, well drained

* * *

Confectioners' Sugar Frosting

In large bowl of electric mixer, thoroughly mix 1¼ cups of the flour, sugar, salt and undissolved yeast. Combine milk, water and margarine in a saucepan. Heat over low heat until liquids are warm (120°). Margarine need not melt. Gradually add to dry ingredients and beat 2 minutes at medium speed, scraping bowl occasionally. Add egg and ¾ cup more flour, or enough flour to make a thick batter. Beat at high speed for 2 minutes, scraping bowl occasionally. Stir in enough of remaining flour to make a stiff batter. Cover bowl tightly with plastic wrap. Refrigerate for at least 2 hours, or up to 3 days.

When ready to shape dough, combine the ½ cup of flour for filling with pecans and brown sugar.

Turn dough out onto lightly floured board and divide in half. Roll half the dough to a 14″ × 7″ rectangle. Spread with ¾ cup of the cherries. Sprinkle with half the brown sugar mixture. Roll up from long side as for jelly roll. Seal edges. Place sealed edge down in a circle on a greased baking sheet. Pinch ends together firmly. Cut slits two-thirds through the ring at 1-inch intervals; turn each 1-inch section on its side. Repeat with remaining dough and filling. Cover; let rise in warm place, free from draft, until doubled in bulk (about 1 hour).

Bake at 375° for about 20 to 25 minutes, or until firm and browned. Remove from baking sheets and cool on wire racks. Frost while still warm with Confectioners' Sugar Frosting. Makes 2 coffee rings.

Confectioners' Sugar Frosting: To 2 cups of sifted confectioners' sugar, gradually add about 2 tablespoons of hot water or milk until the frosting has a good spreading consistency. Stir in 1 teaspoon of vanilla or almond flavoring.

1/12 Recipe, Frosted

Calories	508	Sodium	116 mg.
Carbohydrate	88 Gm.	Potassium	171 mg.
Protein	10 Gm.	Cholesterol	25 mg.
Fat	14 Gm.		

CHAPTER 8

PASTAS AND SUCH

CHAPTER 8

PASTAS AND SUCH

Many of us enjoy a change from potatoes and bread. The pastas—macaroni, spaghetti and noodles—offer a bewildering assortment of shapes and tastes to tempt eye and appetite.

Rice also offers a pleasant alternative, as do dried beans and peas, which provide valuable protein as well as carbohydrate.

If you are wary of eating too much saturated fat, you will avoid sauces which contain much cheese and choose instead those which emphasize vegetable flavors. Some suggestions appear in the following pages.

FOR PERFECT PASTA

To cook 8 ounces (2 cups) of macaroni for 4 servings:

1. In a large saucepot, heat 3 quarts of water to a rapid boil.
2. Add 1 tablespoon of Morton Lite Salt mixture.
3. Gradually add 8 ounces (about 2 cups) of macaroni or spaghetti or 8 ounces (about 4 cups) of egg noodles. (Spaghetti needs special handling: Do a handful at a time, holding one end of the handful until the other end softens, then release. Or break into three sections.) Be sure water continues to boil.
4. Cook, uncovered, stirring occasionally and gently until tender. To test, taste. It should be tender yet firm. Very small pasta cooks in 2 minutes; average is 8 to 10 minutes; some larger shapes require 15 minutes. (Check package directions.)
5. As soon as macaroni is *al dente* (barely tender), turn it into a colander or large strainer. Mix with other ingredients in the recipe and serve at once. Rinsing is considered unnecessary except when the pasta is to be served cold. Then rinse with cold water and drain well.

Per Serving

Calories	203	Sodium	276 mg.
Carbohydrate	41 Gm.	Potassium	100 mg.
Protein	7 Gm.	Cholesterol	0
Fat	1 Gm.		

In general, 8 ounces yield 4 servings. More specific mathematics are:

Product	Dry Weight	Cooked
Elbow macaroni	8 oz. (2 cups)	4½ cups
Spaghetti	8 oz.	5 cups
Egg noodles	8 oz. (about 4 cups)	4 cups

QUICK MARINARA SAUCE

¼ cup vegetable oil
2 cloves garlic, halved
1 can (35 oz.) whole tomatoes, cut up, with liquid
1½ teaspoons Morton Lite
  Salt mixture

⅛ teaspoon pepper
¼ cup chopped parsley
¾ teaspoon basil

Heat oil in medium saucepan. Add garlic and cook gently without browning for about 5 minutes, long enough to scent the oil. Remove garlic. Add tomatoes, salt, pepper, parsley and basil. Cover and simmer 20 minutes. Uncover; cook about 15 minutes longer. Serve over freshly cooked spaghetti. Makes 4 cups, enough for 6 servings.

Per Serving

Calories	116	Sodium	465 mg.
Carbohydrate	6 Gm.	Potassium	645 mg.
Protein	2 Gm.	Cholesterol	0
Fat	10 Gm.		

MUSHROOM SPAGHETTI SAUCE

¼ cup vegetable oil
1 cup chopped onion
1 clove garlic, minced
¾ lb. fresh mushrooms, sliced (about 5 cups)
1 can (1 lb.) whole tomatoes, cut up, with juice
1 can (8 oz.) tomato sauce
1 cup water
2 teaspoons Morton Lite Salt mixture
1 teaspoon sugar
1 teaspoon crushed oregano
1 bay leaf
¼ teaspoon pepper

Heat oil in a very large skillet or Dutch oven. Add onion, garlic and mushrooms. Cook, stirring occasionally, about 10 minutes, or until onion is tender. Add remaining ingredients and stir. Boil gently, uncovered, stirring occasionally, about 1 hour, or until thickened. Remove bay leaf. Serve with freshly cooked spaghetti. Makes 4 cups, about 6 servings.

Per Serving

Calories	181	Sodium	536 mg.
Carbohydrate	13 Gm.	Potassium	1050 mg.
Protein	3 Gm.	Cholesterol	0
Fat	14 Gm.		

ZUCCHINI SPAGHETTI

4 medium zucchini, washed and cut into ¼-inch slices
¼ cup water
1 tablespoon plus 1½ teaspoons Morton Lite Salt mixture
½ cup unsalted polyunsaturated margarine
¼ teaspoon pepper
3 quarts boiling water
8 oz. spaghetti

Place zucchini in saucepan with ¼ cup of water and ½ teaspoon of salt. Bring to boil, cover and reduce heat. Simmer until just tender. Drain, then chop zucchini. Return to saucepan; add margarine, 1 teaspoon of salt and pepper. Simmer about 2 minutes, or until warm through. Add 1 tablespoon of salt to 3 quarts of rapidly boiling water. Gradually add spaghetti so water continues to boil. Cook, uncovered, stirring occasionally, for 8 to 10 minutes, or until tender. When spaghetti is tender, drain in colander and immediately toss with zucchini. Makes 4 servings.

Per Serving

Calories	375	Sodium	417 mg.
Carbohydrate	33 Gm.	Potassium	1850 mg.
Protein	6 Gm.	Cholesterol	0
Fat	25 Gm.		

SPAGHETTI WITH EGGPLANT SAUCE

2 lbs. whole ripe tomatoes, peeled and diced
2 cloves garlic, minced
¼ cup vegetable oil
1 can (6 oz.) tomato paste
⅓ cup cold water
1 small onion, chopped
¼ teaspoon crushed red pepper
¼ teaspoon basil
¼ teaspoon oregano
1 large eggplant, peeled and cubed
¼ cup chopped parsley
12 oz. spaghetti
1½ tablespoons Morton Lite Salt mixture
4 to 5 quarts boiling water

In a Dutch oven or a large saucepan, sauté tomatoes and garlic in 1 tablespoon of the oil for 2 minutes. Stir in tomato paste, water, onion, pepper and herbs. Cover and simmer 2 hours, stirring occasionally, to prevent sticking. Sauté the eggplant in remaining oil until lightly brown and soft, stirring frequently. Add to tomato sauce along with parsley. Cook over low heat for 45 minutes. Near the end of the cooking time, gradually add spaghetti and salt to rapidly boiling water so that water continues to boil. Cook, uncovered, stirring occasionally, until tender (about 10 minutes). Drain in colander. Serve with eggplant sauce. Makes 6 servings.

Per Serving

Calories	367	Sodium	398 mg.
Carbohydrate	59 Gm.	Potassium	1450 mg.
Protein	11 Gm.	Cholesterol	0
Fat	11 Gm.		

SPAGHETTI AND MEATBALLS

1 lb. meat loaf mix (ground beef, pork and veal)
1 slice bread
¼ cup milk
3 small cloves garlic
2 teaspoons chopped parsley
1 tablespoon grated Parmesan cheese
1 egg
1¼ teaspoons Morton Lite Salt mixture
Dash pepper
1 tablespoon vegetable oil
1 can (35 oz.) Italian-style tomatoes, cut up
2 cans (6 oz. each) tomato paste
1 cup water
¼ cup sugar
1 tablespoon instant minced onion
1 tablespoon chopped parsley
1 teaspoon crushed oregano
1 lb. thin spaghetti

Additional grated Parmesan cheese (optional)

Put meat in large bowl. Dip bread in milk; crumble into meat. Add 1 clove of mashed garlic, parsley, grated Parmesan, egg, ¼ teaspoon of the salt and pepper. Mix well. Shape into 12 balls. In large heavy pan, brown meatballs in oil. Remove and set aside. Discard fat. Place tomatoes in pan in which meatballs were browned. Stir in tomato paste, water, sugar, 2 cloves of mashed garlic, onion, parsley, oregano and remaining teaspoon of salt. Bring to boil. Add meatballs. Simmer uncovered for 1 hour, stirring occasionally. Meanwhile, cook spaghetti for 8 to 11 minutes, or until desired tenderness; drain. Serve sauce and meatballs over spaghetti, topping with Parmesan if desired. Serves 4.

Per Serving

Calories	792	Sodium	1883 mg.
Carbohydrate	133 Gm.	Potassium	1931 mg.
Protein	35 Gm.	Cholesterol	146 mg.
Fat	14 Gm.		

POPPYSEED NOODLES

3 quarts rapidly boiling water
8 oz. wide egg noodles (about 4 cups)
1 tablespoon Morton Lite Salt mixture

½ cup unsalted polyunsaturated margarine
2 tablespoons poppyseeds (or sesame seeds)

Bring water to boil, then gradually add noodles and salt so water continues to boil. Cook, uncovered, stirring occasionally, until tender (about 10 minutes). Drain in colander. Meanwhile melt margarine. Add poppyseeds. Cook over low heat for 5 minutes, stirring occasionally. Add noodles and mix well. Makes 4 servings.

Per Serving

Calories	356	Sodium	280 mg.
Carbohydrate	26 Gm.	Potassium	1075 mg.
Protein	5 Gm.	Cholesterol	110 mg.
Fat	26 Gm.		

BEEF AND MACARONI

1 can (4 oz.) sliced mushrooms
¼ cup chopped onion
½ teaspoon crushed oregano
2 tablespoons vegetable oil
1 lb. lean ground beef
1 teaspoon Morton Lite Salt
mixture

¼ teaspoon pepper
¼ teaspoon garlic powder
2 cans (8 oz. each) tomato
sauce
8 oz. (2 cups) elbow macaroni
½ cup shredded sharp Cheddar
cheese (optional)

Drain the mushrooms, reserving the broth. In a large skillet or pot, sauté mushrooms, onion and oregano in oil until onion is crisp-tender. Add beef; scramble and brown
lightly. Stir in salt, pepper, garlic powder, tomato sauce
and reserved mushroom broth. Simmer uncovered for 10
minutes, stirring occasionally. Meanwhile, cook macaroni
for 9 to 12 minutes, to desired tenderness. Drain. Add to
skillet; mix with meat and sauce. If using cheese, sprinkle
it over surface; cover and heat a minute until cheese
melts. Makes 6 servings.

Per Serving

Calories	461	Sodium	421 mg.
Carbohydrate	39 Gm.	Potassium	1198 mg.
Protein	32 Gm.	Cholesterol	84 mg.
Fat	19 Gm.		

ORANGE ALMOND NOODLES

8 oz. egg noodles (about 4
cups)
¼ cup unsalted polyunsaturated margarine, melted
½ cup chopped blanched almonds
1 tablespoon poppyseeds
1 tablespoon grated orange
peel

1 tablespoon grated lemon peel
½ teaspoon Morton Lite Salt
mixture
⅛ teaspoon pepper
* * *
1 cup dairy sour cream (optional)

Cook noodles for 7 to 9 minutes, or to desired tenderness. Meantime, combine margarine, almonds, poppyseeds, orange and lemon peels, salt and pepper. Drain noodles and toss with seasonings. Turn onto a hot platter. If desired, top with spoonfuls of sour cream. Makes 6 servings.

Per Serving

Calories	219	Sodium	109 mg.
Carbohydrate	11 Gm.	Potassium	241 mg.
Protein	3 Gm.	Cholesterol	62 mg.
Fat	18 Gm.		

REALLY GOOD RICE

For about 4 servings of rice, follow these directions:

1. Measure into saucepan 1 cup of regular milled white rice, 2 cups of water and 1 teaspoon of Morton Lite Salt mixture. Place over high heat, and when water boils vigorously, stir several times and cover pan tightly.
2. Turn heat as low as possible and cook for 14 minutes.
3. Turn off heat, lift grains gently with a fork, and allow to steam. Water should be absorbed and grains separate, flaky and tender, with some firmness.

Per Serving

Calories	178	Sodium	278 mg.
Carbohydrate	39 Gm.	Potassium	493 mg.
Protein	3 Gm.	Cholesterol	0
Fat	trace		

For *brown rice,* increase liquid to 2½ cups; cook for 45 minutes. Cook *parboiled rice* 20 minutes. For *precooked rice,* follow directions on package.

1 cup uncooked brown rice yields 4 cups cooked.
1 cup uncooked regular white rice yields 3 cups cooked.
1 cup uncooked parboiled rice yields 4 cups cooked.
1 cup uncooked precooked rice yields a little more than 2 cups cooked.

CURRIED RICE

¼ cup unsalted polyunsaturated margarine
1 cup chopped onion
1 cup chopped green pepper
½ cup dried currants
2 cups uncooked regular rice
  (not precooked)

½ teaspoon curry powder
1 teaspoon Morton Lite Salt
  mixture
¼ teaspoon pepper
1 quart homemade chicken
  broth

Heat margarine in saucepan. Add onion, green pepper and currants, and cook over medium-low heat until onion is tender. Stir in rice and seasonings; cook until golden, not browned. Add broth and mix well. Bring to boil, cover and reduce heat. Simmer for 14 minutes. Remove from heat, toss lightly and serve at once. A nice base for creamed mixtures or a good side dish with chicken. Makes 8 servings.

Per Serving

Calories	264	Sodium	193 mg.
Carbohydrate	44 Gm.	Potassium	287 mg.
Protein	6 Gm.	Cholesterol	10 mg.
Fat	7 Gm.		

RICE WITH SAGE

⅓ cup unsalted polyunsaturated margarine
1 cup uncooked regular rice
  (not precooked)

1 teaspoon Morton Lite Salt
  mixture
2 cups water
¾ cup chopped onion
¼ teaspoon sage

Heat margarine in saucepan. Add rice and salt and cook, stirring constantly over low heat until rice is golden, not browned. Remove from heat. Gradually stir in water; add chopped onion and sage. Bring to boil. Cover; simmer for

12 to 15 minutes, or until all liquid is absorbed. Serve with chicken or pork. Makes 6 servings.

Per Serving

Calories	224	Sodium	189 mg.
Carbohydrate	28 Gm.	Potassium	274 mg.
Protein	3 Gm.	Cholesterol	0
Fat	11 Gm.		

GOLDEN RICE

¼ cup unsalted polyunsaturated margarine
½ cup chopped celery and leaves
1½ tablespoons instant minced onion
1 cup uncooked regular rice (not precooked)
1 teaspoon Morton Lite Salt mixture

1 teaspoon sugar
1 teaspoon grated orange peel
1 cup orange juice
1 cup water
2 oranges, peeled and cut into bite-size pieces (1 cup)
½ cup slivered almonds, toasted
Minced fresh parsley

Heat margarine in saucepan. Add celery and onion and cook until soft. Add rice; cook, stirring frequently, until golden but not brown. Blend in salt, sugar, orange peel, orange juice and water; cover and bring to a boil. Stir once. Reduce heat and simmer, covered, for 20 to 25 minutes, or until tender. Add oranges and almonds; toss lightly to mix. Serve garnished with minced parsley. Makes 6 servings.

Per Serving

Calories	260	Sodium	198 mg.
Carbohydrate	38 Gm.	Potassium	548 mg.
Protein	4 Gm.	Cholesterol	0
Fat	11 Gm.		

SPANISH RICE

½ cup unsalted polyunsaturated margarine
1 cup chopped onion
¾ cup chopped green pepper
⅔ cup uncooked regular rice (not precooked)

½ teaspoon Morton Lite Salt mixture
4 tomatoes, peeled, seeded and quartered
1 bay leaf, crumbled
¼ teaspoon pepper

Melt margarine in medium saucepan. Add other ingredients and mix well. Turn into a 2-quart casserole. Cover. Bake, stirring occasionally, at 350° for about 1½ hours, or until rice is tender. Makes 6 servings.

Per Serving

Calories	280	Sodium	106 mg.
Carbohydrate	30 Gm.	Potassium	570 mg.
Protein	4 Gm.	Cholesterol	0
Fat	17 Gm.		

TOMATO-BAKED BEANS

1 lb. navy (pea) beans
6 cups water
1 small bay leaf
1 can (1 lb.) tomatoes, cut up
½ cup sugar
½ cup chopped onion

1 teaspoon dry mustard
1½ teaspoons Morton Lite Salt mixture
¼ teaspoon pepper
¼ cup unsalted polyunsaturated margarine

Wash and pick over beans. Place them in a saucepan with water and bay leaf. Cover and cook gently until almost tender, about 1¾ hours. Drain, reserving 1½ cups of bean liquid. (If necessary, add water to make 1½ cups.) Grease a 2-quart casserole. In it place cooked beans, bean liquid, tomatoes, sugar, chopped onion, mustard, salt and pepper. Mix well. Dot with margarine. Bake at 325° for 3 hours, or until glazed and very tender. Makes 6 servings.

Per Serving

Calories	410	Sodium	379 mg.
Carbohydrate	65 Gm.	Potassium	150 mg.
Protein	20 Gm.	Cholesterol	0
Fat	10 Gm.		

SOYBEAN BAKE

1½ cups dry soybeans
2 tablespoons unsalted polyunsaturated margarine
½ cup chopped onion
1 teaspoon Morton Lite Salt mixture

¼ teaspoon pepper
¼ cup catsup or Sweet Catsup Sauce (page 95)
¼ cup dark molasses
1 tablespoon dry mustard

Wash soybeans. In saucepan, soak soybeans overnight in water to barely cover. Next day, bring to a boil, cover and simmer until nearly tender (about 3 hours). Toward the end of the cooking period, heat margarine in medium skillet. Add onion and cook over medium heat, stirring, until soft. Season with salt and pepper. Combine cooked beans, onion, catsup, molasses and mustard. Place in 2-quart casserole or bean pot. Bake at 325° for 1 hour, or until done. Cover, but lift lid several times during baking to allow excess liquid to evaporate. Makes 2 quarts.

Per 1 Cup Serving

Calories	213	Sodium	236 mg.
Carbohydrate	17 Gm.	Potassium	458 mg.
Protein	13 Gm.	Cholesterol	0
Fat	10 Gm.		

CHAPTER 9

DESSERTS

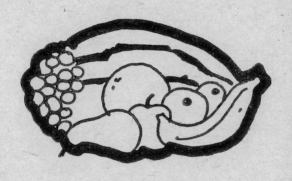

CHAPTER 9

DESSERTS

If we all were models of perfection, only the thinnest of us would eat any dessert except fruit. Desserts as we know them share a common drawback: they are high in calories and therefore must be carefully selected.

If you are fighting the battle of the bulge, be wary. Serve fruit desserts as often as possible, milk desserts next most frequently, and only occasionally plan on cookies, pies and cakes.

Each of the recipes in this chapter is thoughtfully selected and tested to solve a problem.

Margarine or oil is used instead of shortening in most cases, since this is one technique for reducing saturated fat content. And eggs are few and far between, since yolks contain cholesterol. (Remember, however, egg whites are cholesterol-free and are good protein food.)

You'll find lots of satisfying sweets in the pages ahead. Sweet fruit, temptingly hot, is particularly appealing when the thermometer plunges and chill winds blow. When possible, bake dessert with the meat course to save energy.

APPLE BROWN BETTY

¼ cup melted unsalted polyunsaturated margarine
1½ cups day-old bread cubes
4 to 5 cups sliced tart apples
¾ cup brown sugar

1 teaspoon cinnamon
¼ teaspoon Morton Lite Salt
  mixture
2 tablespoons lemon juice
⅓ cup water

Mix melted margarine with bread cubes. Combine the apples with sugar, cinnamon and salt. Place one-third of the bread cubes in the bottom of a greased 2-quart casserole. Cover with half the apples. Repeat, then top that layer with last third of bread cubes. Combine lemon juice and water and pour over all. Cover. Bake at 350° for 30 minutes. Uncover; bake 30 minutes more. Makes 6 servings.

Per Serving

Calories	240	Sodium	55 mg.
Carbohydrate	54 Gm.	Potassium	250 mg.
Protein	2 Gm.	Cholesterol	0
Fat	4 Gm.		

APPLE CRISP

6 to 7 tart apples (about 2 lbs.)
2 tablespoons lemon juice
1 tablespoon grated lemon peel
1 cup sugar

¾ cup flour
⅓ cup chopped pecans
1 tablespoon cinnamon
¼ cup unsalted polyunsaturated margarine

Peel, core and slice apples. Place half the slices in a 9-inch-square pan; sprinkle with half the lemon juice and half the peel. Combine remaining ingredients, mixing thoroughly. Sprinkle half over apples. Repeat layers, ending with sugar-flour mixture. Bake at 375° for 35 minutes. Increase temperature to 400° and bake 10 minutes more. Makes 9 servings.

Per Serving

Calories	265	Sodium	3 mg.
Carbohydrate	48 Gm.	Potassium	244 mg.
Protein	2 Gm.	Cholesterol	0
Fat	9 Gm.		

EASY APPLE-NOODLE BAKE

6 oz. wide egg noodles (about 3 cups)
1 tablespoon Morton Lite Salt mixture
3 to 4 quarts boiling water
¼ cup unsalted polyunsaturated margarine, softened
¼ cup granulated sugar
¼ cup orange juice

1 can (21 oz.) apple pie filling
1 medium apple, sliced
¼ cup dark seedless raisins
¼ cup golden raisins
¾ cup corn flakes, crushed, or ¼ cup corn flake crumbs
¼ cup firmly packed light brown sugar

Gradually add noodles and salt to rapidly boiling water so that water continues to boil. Cook, uncovered, stirring occasionally, until tender. Drain in colander. Add margarine to hot noodles and toss until melted. Add all remaining ingredients except corn flakes and brown sugar; toss gently until combined. Turn mixture into shallow 1½-quart casserole. Mix crushed corn flakes and brown sugar; sprinkle over surface of pudding. Bake uncovered at 350° for 35 to 40 minutes, or until apples are tender. Serve warm. Makes 6 servings.

Per Serving

Calories	397	Sodium	224 mg.
Carbohydrate	66 Gm.	Potassium	867 mg.
Protein	6 Gm.	Cholesterol	110 mg.
Fat	13 Gm.		

BROILED BANANAS IN SOUR CREAM

4 firm bananas
⅔ cup dairy sour cream

⅓ cup brown sugar

Peel bananas and cut in half lengthwise. Place in a shallow baking dish. Spoon sour cream over bananas. Sprinkle with brown sugar. Place under broiler. Broil for 3 to 5 minutes, until bananas are just tender. Makes 4 servings.

Per Serving

Calories	244	Sodium	8 mg.
Carbohydrate	61 Gm.	Potassium	450 mg.
Protein	2 Gm.	Cholesterol	3 mg.
Fat	1 Gm.		

MAPLE-BAKED PEARS

3 large, firm, fresh pears, pared, halved and cored
2 tablespoons lemon juice

2 tablespoons unsalted polyunsaturated margarine
6 tablespoons maple syrup
½ cup boiling water

Brush pears with lemon juice. Arrange in a shallow baking dish. Place 1 teaspoon of margarine and 1½ teaspoons of maple syrup in each pear half. Mix remaining 3 tablespoons of syrup with water and pour into bottom of dish. Bake at 400° for 1 hour, or until tender, basting occasionally with pan liquid. Makes 6 servings.

Per Serving

Calories	119	Sodium	6 mg.
Carbohydrate	21 Gm.	Potassium	125 mg.
Protein	trace	Cholesterol	0
Fat	4 Gm.		

BANANAS AFLAME

¼ cup unsalted polyunsaturated margarine
½ cup light brown sugar
1 tablespoon lemon juice

4 green-tipped bananas, peeled and halved lengthwise
⅓ cup Cointreau

Melt margarine in blazer pan of chafing dish. Stir in brown sugar; heat until well blended. Sprinkle lemon juice over bananas; add bananas to margarine–sugar mixture. Continue to cook, carefully turning bananas until they are glazed and softened (3 to 5 minutes). Pour Cointreau evenly over bananas. Bring to a boil. Ignite with long match. Serve after flames die. Makes 4 servings.

Per Serving

Calories	373	Sodium	10 mg.
Carbohydrate	69 Gm.	Potassium	375 mg.
Protein	2 Gm.	Cholesterol	0
Fat	13 Gm.		

CHERRY COBBLER

1 can (1 lb.) red sour cherries packed in water
½ cup sugar
1 tablespoon cornstarch
2 teaspoons unsalted polyunsaturated margarine

1 teaspoon lemon juice
3 drops red food coloring

* * *

1 recipe Cobbler Dough (below)

Drain cherries, reserving ¾ cup of juice. In a small saucepan over medium heat, mix together sugar, cornstarch and cherry juice until smooth. Bring to a boil, stirring constantly, and boil for 1 minute. Stir in margarine, lemon juice and food coloring. Remove from heat. Add cherries. Pour into baking dish approximately 10″ × 6″ × 1¾″. Drop Cobbler Dough by teaspoonsful onto hot cherry mixture. Bake at 400° for 20 minutes. Makes 8 servings.

Cobbler Dough:

1 cup sifted flour
1 tablespoon sugar
2 teaspoons baking powder
¼ teaspoon Morton Lite Salt mixture

¼ teaspoon nutmeg
¼ cup vegetable oil
⅓ cup milk

Sift together flour, sugar, baking powder, salt and nutmeg into medium bowl. Stir in oil. Add milk and mix well.

Per Serving

Calories	208	Sodium	166 mg.
Carbohydrate	31 Gm.	Potassium	150 mg.
Protein	2 Gm.	Cholesterol	1 mg.
Fat	9 Gm.		

MERINGUED PEARS

2 cans (16 oz. each) pear halves
⅓ cup pear syrup
3 tablespoons brown sugar
1 teaspoon grated lemon peel
½ teaspoon nutmeg

2 egg whites
Dash Morton Lite Salt mixture
2 tablespoons confectioners' sugar
2 tablespoons chopped almonds

Drain pears, reserving syrup. Place pear halves, cut side up, in 10-inch baking dish or pie pan. Pour ⅓ cup of pear syrup over bottom of pan. Combine brown sugar, lemon peel and nutmeg. Sprinkle this mixture evenly over pear halves. Beat egg whites and salt until almost stiff. Gradually add confectioners' sugar, continuing to beat until stiff. Pile meringue evenly over pear halves. Sprinkle meringue with chopped almonds. Bake at 325° for 15 to 20 minutes. Serve warm. Makes 8 servings.

Per Serving

Calories	120	Sodium	48 mg.
Carbohydrate	28 Gm.	Potassium	200 mg.
Protein	1 Gm.	Cholesterol	0
Fat	0		

A cold fruit dessert seems just right when the main course has been a bit heavy or rich. Many require little preparation time. For additional advice on fruits, consult the chapter on salads.

BANANA FRUIT CUPS

This recipe calls for a combination of fresh and/or canned fruits, dressed with a flavorful sugar syrup. Make the syrup in advance and combine the fruits with the syrup just before serving. Try sliced bananas with a choice of:

Red grapes, cubed pears
Cubed avocado, whole cranberry sauce
Mandarin orange sections, green grapes
Grapefruit and orange sections
Pineapple chunks, cubed apple
Apricot halves, green grapes

The flavored syrups which follow call for this recipe as an ingredient:

SIMPLE SYRUP

1½ cups sugar   2 cups water

In a saucepan, combine sugar and water and bring to a boil, stirring constantly. Reduce heat and simmer for 5 minutes. Cool. Makes 3 cups.

Per Recipe

Calories	1155	Sodium	0
Carbohydrate	298 Gm.	Potassium	0
Protein	0	Cholesterol	0
Fat	0		

ORANGE RUM SYRUP

1½ cups Simple Syrup   ¼ cup orange juice
¼ teaspoon grated orange   2 tablespoons lime juice
  peel   1 teaspoon rum

Mix and chill. Makes 2 cups.

Per Serving

Calories	1221	Sodium	2 mg.
Carbohydrate	311 Gm.	Potassium	250 mg.
Protein	1 Gm.	Cholesterol	0
Fat	trace		

LIME-LEMON SYRUP

1½ cups Simple Syrup   4 teaspoons lemon juice
2 tablespoons lime juice   Pinch of Morton Lite Salt mixture

Mix and chill. Makes 1⅔ cups.

Per Recipe

Calories	1168	Sodium	133 mg.
Carbohydrate	303 Gm.	Potassium	180 mg.
Protein	trace	Cholesterol	0
Fat	0		

SPIRITED SYRUP

1½ cups Simple Syrup

2 tablespoons green crème de menthe, cream sherry or brandy

Mix and chill. Makes 1⅔ cups.

Per Recipe

Calories	1238	Sodium	1 mg.
Carbohydrate	306 Gm.	Potassium	0
Protein	0	Cholesterol	0
Fat	0		

BANANA MERINGUES

First prepare the meringues:
4 egg whites
⅛ teaspoon Morton Lite Salt mixture
¼ teaspoon cream of tartar

1 cup sugar
½ teaspoon vanilla
1 tablespoon grated orange peel

In large bowl, beat egg whites, salt and cream of tartar until foamy. Gradually beat in sugar, 1 tablespoon at a time, and continue beating until stiff peaks form when beater is withdrawn. Fold in vanilla and orange peel. Spoon 6 mounds onto greased baking sheet and make a depression in center of each mound. Bake at 225° for 45 minutes, or until lightly browned. Remove and cool. Several hours before serving, prepare:

Orange-Banana Filling:
3 tablespoons cornstarch
⅓ cup sugar
¼ teaspoon Morton Lite Salt mixture

1 cup water
¾ cup orange juice
1 teaspoon grated orange peel
3 bananas

In medium saucepan, mix cornstarch, sugar and salt. Gradually stir in water and orange juice. Place over low heat; stir constantly until mixture thickens and comes to a boil. Simmer for 1 minute, continuing to stir. Remove from heat; stir in orange peel. Cool. Peel bananas; slice. Fold in. Chill about 3 hours. Makes 6 servings.

Per Serving

Calories	139	Sodium	53 mg.
Carbohydrate	33 Gm.	Potassium	321 mg.
Protein	2 Gm.	Cholesterol	0
Fat	0		

HONEYDEW TROPICALE

3 cups honeydew melon balls
2 cups fresh orange sections
6 tablespoons lemon juice

2 tablespoons lime juice
¼ cup sugar

In a large bowl, mix honeydew and oranges. Combine lemon and lime juices with sugar; pour over fruit. Cover and chill. Serve in sherbet glasses. Makes 6 servings.

Per Serving

Calories	48	Sodium	7 mg.
Carbohydrate	12 Gm.	Potassium	341 mg.
Protein	trace	Cholesterol	0
Fat	trace		

Gelatin desserts can be prepared early in the day or even the night before you plan to serve them. Always cool and refreshing, they can also present the food values of fruit in a different way.

MOLDED SUMMER FRUIT

2 envelopes unflavored gelatin
⅔ cup sugar
⅛ teaspoon Morton Lite Salt mixture
2¾ cups cold water

½ cup lime or lemon juice
4 cups mixed fresh fruit (peach slices, halved white grapes, watermelon pieces and cantaloupe balls)

Mix together gelatin, sugar and salt in saucepan. Stir in 1 cup of the water. Place over low heat; stir constantly until gelatin and sugar are dissolved (4 to 5 minutes). Remove from heat. Add remaining 1¾ cups of water, and lime or lemon juice. Arrange a small amount of the fruit in the bottom of the mold to form a design. Spoon on just enough of the gelatin mixture to cover bottom of mold; chill until almost firm. Chill remaining gelatin mixture until it is the consistency of unbeaten egg white; fold in remaining fruit. Spoon on top of almost firm layer; chill until firm. Unmold. Makes 10 servings.

Per Serving

Calories	91	Sodium	20 mg.
Carbohydrate	19 Gm.	Potassium	115 mg.
Protein	4 Gm.	Cholesterol	0
Fat	trace		

FRUIT JUICE SNOW

1 envelope unflavored gelatin
½ cup sugar
⅛ teaspoon Morton Lite Salt mixture
1¼ cups water

1 can (6 oz.) frozen fruit concentrate of choice (except pineapple juice)
2 egg whites

In a small saucepan, thoroughly mix gelatin, sugar and salt. Add ½ cup of the water. Place over low heat, stirring constantly until gelatin is dissolved. Remove from heat and stir in remaining ¾ cup of water and the fruit juice concentrate. Stir until melted. Chill until slightly thicker than the consistency of unbeaten egg white. Turn into small bowl of electric mixer. Add unbeaten egg whites and beat until mixture begins to hold its shape. (Or you may use rotary beater, beating until mixture is light and fluffy—about 7 minutes. Hand beating will go faster if bowl is placed in a large bowl of ice and water.) Spoon into dessert dishes and chill until firm. Serve plain or with Melba Sauce (page 196). Makes 8 servings.

Per Serving

Calories	76	Sodium	30 mg.
Carbohydrate	17 Gm.	Potassium	208 mg.
Protein	2 Gm.	Cholesterol	0
Fat	trace		

STRAWBERRY SNOW

1 envelope unflavored gelatin	⅛ teaspoon Morton Lite Salt
½ cup cold water	mixture
1 package (10 oz.) frozen	1 teaspoon grated lemon peel
strawberries, thawed	1 teaspoon lemon juice
½ cup sugar	2 egg whites

Sprinkle gelatin over cold water in saucepan. Place over low heat; stir constantly until gelatin dissolves (about 3 minutes). Remove from heat. Purée strawberries in electric blender or by rubbing through a sieve. Add to dissolved gelatin with sugar, salt, lemon peel and juice. Chill, stirring occasionally until mixture mounds slightly when dropped from a spoon. Add to unbeaten egg whites in chilled bowl and beat at high speed of electric mixer until mixture is light and fluffy and mounds when beater is lifted (7 to 10 minutes). Turn into 1-quart bowl or mold or into individual dessert dishes. Chill until set (2 or 3 hours). Makes 10 servings.

Per Serving

Calories	70	Sodium	24 mg.
Carbohydrate	16 Gm.	Potassium	52 mg.
Protein	1 Gm.	Cholesterol	0
Fat	trace		

PINEAPPLE WHIP

1 envelope unflavored gelatin	1¾ cups canned pineapple
⅓ cup sugar	juice
⅛ teaspoon Morton Lite Salt	½ teaspoon grated lemon
mixture	peel

Mix gelatin, sugar and salt thoroughly in a small saucepan. Add ½ cup of the pineapple juice. Place over low heat, stirring constantly, until gelatin is dissolved. Remove from heat and stir in remaining pineapple juice and lemon peel. Chill until slightly thicker than the consistency of unbeaten egg white. Beat with a rotary beater or electric mixer until light and fluffy and double in volume. Spoon into dessert dishes and chill until firm. Makes 6 servings.

Pineapple Whip: Per Serving

Calories	83	Sodium	25 mg.
Carbohydrate	19 Gm.	Potassium	160 mg.
Protein	2 Gm.	Cholesterol	0
Fat	trace		

Orange Whip: Use orange juice instead of pineapple juice.
Apricot Whip: Instead of pineapple juice, use 1½ cups of apricot nectar and ¼ cup of water.
Coffee Whip: Substitute 1⅔ cups of cold strong coffee for the pineapple juice. Omit the lemon peel and stir in 1 teaspoon of vanilla with the second addition of coffee.

Orange Whip: Per Serving

Calories	80	Sodium	24 mg.
Carbohydrate	18 Gm.	Potassium	177 mg.
Protein	2 Gm.	Cholesterol	0
Fat	0		

Apricot Whip: Per Serving

Calories	89	Sodium	24 mg.
Carbohydrate	21 Gm.	Potassium	116 mg.
Protein	2 Gm.	Cholesterol	0
Fat	trace		

Coffee Whip: Per Serving

Calories	49	Sodium	25 mg.
Carbohydrate	11 Gm.	Potassium	52 mg.
Protein	2 Gm.	Cholesterol	0
Fat	trace		

SPICY APPLE SPONGE

1 envelope unflavored gelatin
¼ cup cold water
1 cup very hot orange juice
1½ teaspoons vanilla
¼ teaspoon mace
⅛ teaspoon Morton Lite Salt
mixture

½ cup coarsely shredded
peeled apple
1 tablespoon lemon juice
2 egg whites
2 tablespoons sugar

In a medium bowl, sprinkle gelatin over cold water and let stand to soften for 5 minutes. Stir in hot orange juice, mixing until gelatin is dissolved. Add vanilla, mace and salt. Chill until mixture is a little thicker than unbeaten egg whites. Beat until fluffy. Combine apple with lemon juice and fold in. Beat egg whites until soft peaks form. Gradually beat in sugar and beat until stiff peaks form when beater is withdrawn. Fold into apple mixture. Spoon into dessert dishes. Chill about 3 hours, serve cold. Makes 6 servings.

Per Serving

Calories	55	Sodium	41 mg.
Carbohydrate	11 Gm.	Potassium	138 mg.
Protein	3 Gm.	Cholesterol	0
Fat	trace		

You don't need an ice cream freezer to make this sherbet—just your food freezer and a rotary beater.

BUTTERMILK LEMON SHERBET

1 quart buttermilk
1 tablespoon grated lemon peel
¼ cup lemon juice

⅓ cup sugar
1½ cups light corn syrup

Turn buttermilk into large mixing bowl. Add remaining ingredients and stir until well blended. Pour into freezing tray or loaf pan. Freeze quickly until mixture is a mush (about 1 hour). Meantime, chill the mixing bowl. Turn mixture into chilled bowl and beat with rotary beater until smooth. Return to tray and freeze until firm (about 3 hours). Makes about 1 quart.

Per ½ Cup Serving

Calories	365	Sodium	215 mg.
Carbohydrate	64 Gm.	Potassium	150 mg
Protein	8 Gm.	Cholesterol	6 mg.
Fat	0		

Fruit sauces dress up simple puddings and cakes.

WARM LEMON SAUCE

¾ cup sugar
2 tablespoons cornstarch
¼ teaspoon Morton Lite Salt mixture
⅛ teaspoon nutmeg
⅓ cup lemon juice

2 tablespoons unsalted polyunsaturated margarine
1½ cups boiling water
Few drops yellow food coloring
2 teaspoons grated lemon peel

In saucepan, combine sugar, cornstarch, salt and nutmeg; gradually add lemon juice, stirring until smooth. Add margarine and boiling water. Bring to a boil over medium heat, stirring constantly. Boil for 2 minutes. Stir in food coloring, then lemon peel. Serve warm. Makes 2 cups.

Per Recipe

Calories	871	Sodium	279 mg.
Carbohydrate	170 Gm.	Potassium	350 mg.
Protein	trace	Cholesterol	0
Fat	25 Gm.		

CALIFORNIA ORANGE SAUCE

½ cup sugar
3 tablespoons cornstarch
¼ teaspoon Morton Lite Salt mixture
1 cup orange juice
1 cup boiling water

1 tablespoon grated orange peel
2 large oranges, peeled, cut into bite-size pieces and well drained (about 3⅓ cups)

In a saucepan, combine sugar, cornstarch and salt; gradually add orange juice, stirring until smooth. Add boiling water; bring to a boil over medium heat, stirring constantly. Boil for 2 to 3 minutes; stir in orange peel and orange pieces. Good warm or cool. Makes 2⅓ cups.

Per Recipe

Calories	702	Sodium	279 mg.
Carbohydrate	178 Gm.	Potassium	1600 mg.
Protein	5 Gm.	Cholesterol	0
Fat	1 Gm.		

MELBA SAUCE

1 package (10 oz.) frozen raspberries, thawed
½ cup currant jelly

2 teaspoons cornstarch
1 tablespoon cold water

Combine raspberries and jelly in saucepan; boil over medium heat. Blend cornstarch with cold water, add to raspberries. Continue cooking, stirring constantly, until mixture is clear. Makes 1½ cups.

Per Recipe

Calories	419	Sodium	6 mg.
Carbohydrate	104 Gm.	Potassium	300 mg.
Protein	4 Gm.	Cholesterol	0
Fat	trace		

AUSTRIAN CRESCENTS

1 cup walnuts
1 cup unsalted polyunsaturated margarine, softened
¾ cup sugar

1 teaspoon cinnamon
2 teaspoons vanilla
2½ cups sifted flour
1 cup sifted confectioners' sugar

Grind walnuts fine in an electric blender or food grinder. Combine the ground walnuts, margarine, sugar, cinnamon and vanilla; mix well. Add flour and blend into a smooth dough. Wrap dough in foil or plastic film and chill about 3 hours, or until firm. Using a rounded teaspoonful for each cookie, shape dough into crescents. Place on ungreased cookie sheets. Bake at 350° for 15 minutes, or until pale gold. Cool slightly. Gently dip into confectioners' sugar. Cool on racks. Makes about 5 dozen.

Per Crescent

Calories	77	Sodium	trace
Carbohydrates	9 Gm.	Potassium	10 mg.
Protein	trace	Cholesterol	0
Fat	4 Gm.		

ALMOND SQUARES

¾ cup unsalted polyunsaturated margarine, softened
½ cup sugar
2 cups sifted flour

1 tablespoon grated blanched almonds
½ teaspoon Morton Lite Salt mixture
¼ cup blanched whole almonds

Beat together margarine and sugar until blended. Add flour, grated almonds and salt; mix until smooth. Press into a rectangle about 14″ × 6″ × ¼″ on an ungreased baking sheet. Arrange whole almonds in rows over top. Bake at 325° for 30 minutes. Remove from oven and cut into 2″ × 2″ pieces. Makes 21 squares.

Per Square

Calories	122	Sodium	27 mg.
Carbohydrate	13 Gm.	Potassium	69 mg.
Protein	1 Gm.	Cholesterol	0
Fat	7 Gm.		

This do-ahead dessert, although made of simple foods, is a good one to serve at parties.

VANILLA TRIFLE

2 packages (4 servings each) vanilla pudding and pie-filling mix
1 quart milk
2 tablespoons sugar
1 tablespoon vanilla
1 package (3 oz.) ladyfingers
⅓ cup strawberry preserves
½ cup macaroon or vanilla wafer crumbs

In a medium saucepan, combine pudding mix, milk and sugar; mix well. Cook over medium heat, stirring constantly until mixture thickens and comes to a boil. Cool. Stir in vanilla. Split ladyfingers. Fill with preserves and put together again. In a 2-quart serving dish, place a layer of one-fourth of the ladyfingers, cookie crumbs and pudding. Repeat three times, ending with pudding. Refrigerate for 3 hours. Garnish with additional dots of strawberry preserves. Makes 10 servings.

Per Serving

Calories	222	Sodium	143 mg.
Carbohydrate	40 Gm.	Potassium	202 mg.
Protein	5 Gm.	Cholesterol	51 mg.
Fat	5 Gm.		

OATMEAL DROP COOKIES

2 cups sifted flour
1¼ cups sugar
1 teaspoon baking powder
1 teaspoon Morton Lite Salt mixture
1 teaspoon cinnamon
½ teaspoon baking soda
3 cups old-fashioned or quick-cooking oatmeal
1 cup raisins
1 cup vegetable oil
2 eggs
½ cup milk

In a large bowl, stir together flour, sugar, baking powder, salt, cinnamon and baking soda. Mix in oatmeal and raisins. Add oil, eggs and milk, stirring until thoroughly blended. Drop by teaspoonsful 1½ inches apart onto ungreased baking sheet. Bake at 400° for 10 to 12 minutes, or until browned. Makes about 6 dozen.

Calories	77	Sodium	19 mg.
Carbohydrate	10 Gm.	Potassium	34 mg.
Protein	1 Gm.	Cholesterol	8 mg.
Fat	4 Gm.		

OATMEAL FUDGE COOKIES

2 cups sugar
½ cup cocoa powder
½ cup unsalted polyunsaturated margarine
½ cup milk
½ teaspoon Morton Lite Salt mixture

3 cups quick-cooking oatmeal
1 cup chopped walnuts
1 teaspoon cinnamon
½ teaspoon nutmeg
1 teaspoon vanilla
2 eggs, beaten

In a large saucepan, combine sugar, cocoa, margarine, milk and salt; mix well. Stir and cook over medium heat for 3 to 4 minutes. Remove from heat and stir in oatmeal, walnuts, cinnamon, nutmeg and vanilla; mix well. Blend in eggs. Drop by teaspoonsful, 2 inches apart, onto lightly greased cookie sheets. Bake at 350° for 15 minutes. Immediately remove from cookie sheets to wire cooling racks. Makes about 6 dozen.

Per Cookie

Calories	61	Sodium	11 mg.
Carbohydrate	8 Gm.	Potassium	51 mg.
Protein	1 Gm.	Cholesterol	8 mg.
Fat	3 Gm.		

BUTTERSCOTCH BROWNIES

1 cup dark brown sugar
¼ cup vegetable oil
1 egg
½ cup chopped nuts
1 teaspoon vanilla

¾ cup unsifted flour
1 teaspoon baking powder
½ teaspoon Morton Lite Salt mixture

Grease an 8-inch-square baking pan. In a large bowl, stir together brown sugar, oil and egg until smooth. Mix in nuts and vanilla. Mix together flour, baking powder and salt. Add to oil mixture, mixing well. Turn into prepared pan and spread evenly. Bake at 350° for 25 minutes, or until browned. Cut into squares while warm. Makes 16.

Per Serving

Calories	158	Sodium	42 mg.
Carbohydrate	16 Gm.	Potassium	116 mg.
Protein	2 Gm.	Cholesterol	17 mg.
Fat	10 Gm.		

DATE AND NUT BARS

¾ cup sifted flour
1 cup sugar
¼ teaspoon baking powder
⅛ teaspoon Morton Lite Salt mixture
½ cup vegetable oil

2 eggs
½ teaspoon vanilla
1 cup firmly packed finely cut dates
1 cup chopped nuts

Grease an 8- or 9-inch-square baking pan. Sift together flour, sugar, baking powder and salt into mixing bowl. Make a well in the center. Add oil, eggs and vanilla; beat until smooth. Mix in dates and nuts. Turn into baking pan. Bake at 350° for 35 to 40 minutes, or until lightly browned. Cut into bars while still warm. Makes 24.

Per Serving

Calories	147	Sodium	11 mg.
Carbohydrate	17 Gm.	Potassium	187 mg.
Protein	2 Gm.	Cholesterol	23 mg.
Fat	8 Gm.		

CHOCOLATE POPCORN BALLS

1¼ cups sugar
¾ cup light corn syrup
½ cup cocoa powder
2 teaspoons cider vinegar
⅛ teaspoon Morton Lite Salt mixture

2 tablespoons unsalted polyunsaturated margarine
¼ cup evaporated milk
2 quarts unsalted popped corn

In a heavy saucepan, combine sugar, syrup, cocoa powder, vinegar and salt. Add margarine; cook slowly, stirring constantly, until the sugar dissolves. Bring to a boil; slowly add evaporated milk so boiling does not stop. Cook over low heat, stirring occasionally, until mixture reaches 250° on a candy thermometer. Drizzle over popped corn, mixing rapidly. Dip out large spoonfuls and shape into balls. (It helps to wet the hands or rub them lightly with margarine.) Makes ten 4-inch balls.

Per Serving

Calories	217	Sodium	28 mg.
Carbohydrate	50 Gm.	Potassium	130 mg.
Protein	1 Gm.	Cholesterol	trace
Fat	2 Gm.		

OIL PASTRY

For one-crust pie:
1⅓ cups sifted flour
½ teaspoon Morton Lite Salt mixture

⅓ cup vegetable oil
2 tablespoons cold water

In medium bowl, mix flour and salt. Mix in oil with fork. Sprinkle all the water on top; mix well. Press firmly into ball with hands. (Dough may need another tablespoon or two of vegetable oil.) Chill. Flatten dough slightly and roll out between 2 sheets of waxed paper to 12-inch circle. Peel off top paper; place in 9-inch pie pan, paper side up. Peel off paper and fit pastry loosely into pan. Flute edge. If shell is to be baked before filling, prick thoroughly and bake at 450° for 12 to 15 minutes, or until golden brown. If shell and filling are to be baked together, don't prick shell and follow baking directions with filling.

Two-crust pie:

2 cups sifted flour   ½ cup vegetable oil
1 teaspoon Morton Lite Salt   3 tablespoons cold water
  mixture

Follow directions above to prepare dough. Divide dough
almost in half. Flatten larger portion slightly. Follow directions above to roll out in waxed paper and fit into pie
pan. Trim dough ½ inch beyond rim of pan. Roll out remaining dough for top crust. Peel off paper and cut slits to
permit steam to escape during baking; place over filling.
Trim ½ inch beyond rim of pan. Fold edges of both crusts
under; seal and flute. Bake according to filling used.

Per Recipe

	One-Crust	Two-Crust
Calories	910	1304
Carbohydrate	111 Gm.	167 Gm.
Protein	15 Gm.	23 Gm.
Fat	43 Gm.	58 Gm.
Sodium	553 mg.	1104 mg.
Potassium	958 mg.	1680 mg.
Cholesterol	0	0

MARGARINE PASTRY NO. 1

2 cups unsifted flour   ⅔ cup unsalted polyunsatu-
1 teaspoon Morton Lite Salt   rated margarine
  mixture   7 to 9 tablespoons ice water

Measure flour and salt into bowl. Cut in margarine with
pastry blender or 2 knives until mixture resembles coarse
meal. Stir in ice water with fork; mix well. Divide dough
almost in half, shaping into balls. On floured board, roll
out larger ball for bottom crust, smaller ball for top. Bake
as directed in recipe. Enough for 2-crust pie.

Per Recipe

Calories	1160	Sodium	1109 mg.
Carbohydrate	167 Gm.	Potassium	1800 mg.
Protein	23 Gm.	Cholesterol	0
Fat	43 Gm.		

MARGARINE PASTRY NO. 2

1⅓ cups sifted flour
⅛ teaspoon Morton Lite Salt mixture

½ cup unsalted polyunsaturated margarine
3 tablespoons cold water

Mix flour and salt. With pastry blender or 2 knives, cut in margarine until mixture is well blended and fine crumbs form. Sprinkle water over mixture while tossing to blend well. Press dough firmly into ball. Flatten slightly and roll out to 12-inch circle on lightly floured board. Fit loosely into 9-inch pie pan. Trim and flute edge. If shell is to be baked unfilled, prick all over with fork. Bake at 450° for 12 to 15 minutes, or until light golden brown. Cool. If shell is to be baked filled, follow directions with filling. Makes one 9-inch shell.

Per Recipe

Calories	550	Sodium	135 mg.
Carbohydrate	111 Gm.	Potassium	400 mg.
Protein	15 Gm.	Cholesterol	0
Fat	4 Gm.		

DEEP-DISH PEACH PIE

1 recipe Margarine Pastry No. 2 (see above)
3 lbs. peaches (12 medium) or nectarines
½ cup light brown sugar
3 tablespoons cornstarch

¼ teaspoon Morton Lite Salt mixture
½ cup light corn syrup
2 tablespoons unsalted polyunsaturated margarine

Prepare pastry as directed. Roll it out ¼ inch wider than a baking dish 10″ × 6″ × 2″, or a 1½-quart casserole. Pare and slice peaches. Combine brown sugar, cornstarch and salt; stir in corn syrup. Lightly toss with peaches. Turn into baking dish and dot with margarine. Place dough over peaches, letting it extend up the sides of the dish. Bake at 425° for 40 minutes, or until peaches are tender and crust is lightly browned. Makes 8 servings.

Per 1/7 Recipe

Calories	306	Sodium	64 mg.
Carbohydrate	66 Gm.	Potassium	614 mg.
Protein	3 Gm.	Cholesterol	0
Fat	4 Gm.		

CHERRY PIE

Pastry for two-crust pie:
2 cans (1 lb. each) red sour cherries packed in water
3 tablespoons cornstarch
⅔ cup sugar
½ teaspoon Morton Lite Salt mixture
2 tablespoons unsalted polyunsaturated margarine
1 teaspoon lemon juice
¼ teaspoon red food coloring

Prepare pastry. Roll out bottom crust, fitting into 9-inch pan. Allow 1 inch overhang. Roll out top crust and set aside. Drain cherries, reserving 1 cup of juice. In a saucepan, mix together cornstarch, sugar, salt and 1 cup of cherry juice until smooth. Place over medium heat and cook, stirring constantly, until mixture comes to a boil and boils 1 minute. Remove from heat. Stir in margarine, lemon juice, food coloring and cherries. Pour into pastry-lined pan. Cover with top crust. Seal and flute edge. Make several slits in top crust to permit escape of steam. Bake at 425° for 35 to 40 minutes, or until crust is golden brown. Makes one 9-inch pie.

Per 1/7 Recipe

Calories	331	Sodium	239 mg.
Carbohydrate	58 Gm.	Potassium	171 mg.
Protein	4 Gm.	Cholesterol	0
Fat	10 Gm.		

MAPLE APPLE PIE

Pastry for two-crust pie:
6 cups sliced pared apples
1 cup maple syrup
2 tablespoons flour
1 teaspoon cinnamon
½ teaspoon Morton Lite Salt mixture
2 tablespoons unsalted polyunsaturated margarine
Milk

Prepare pastry. Roll out bottom crust, fitting into 9-inch pan. Allow 1 inch overhang. Roll out top crust and set aside. Arrange apples into lined pie plate. Combine syrup, flour, cinnamon and salt. Pour over apples. Dot top with margarine. Cut slits in top crust to permit escape of steam.

Cover pie. Seal and flute edges. Brush pie with a little milk. Place pie pan on a cookie sheet in oven. Bake at 425° for about 50 minutes, or until nicely browned. Makes one 9-inch pie.

Per 1/7 Recipe

Calories	417	Sodium	248 mg.
Carbohydrate	79 Gm.	Potassium	343 mg.
Protein	4 Gm.	Cholesterol	0
Fat	11 Gm.		

HOME-STYLE PEAR PIE

Pastry for two-crust pie:
6 cups (6 medium) sliced pears
2 tablespoons lemon juice
¼ cup flour

¾ cup sugar
¼ teaspoon mace
¼ teaspoon cinnamon
2 tablespoons unsalted polyunsaturated margarine

Prepare pastry. Roll out bottom crust fitting into 9-inch pan. Allow 1 inch overhang. Roll out top crust and set aside. Core unpeeled pears and slice into eighths. Sprinkle with lemon juice, tossing to mix. Mix flour, sugar and spices. Toss with pears to coat lightly. Turn into pastry-lined pan. Dot with margarine. Make slits in top crust and cover pears. Seal and flute. Bake at 425° for 40 to 50 minutes, or until attractively browned. Good with Cheddar cheese. Makes one 9-inch pie.

Per 1/7 Recipe

Calories	439	Sodium	164 mg.
Carbohydrate	84 Gm.	Potassium	434 mg.
Protein	8 Gm.	Cholesterol	0
Fat	11 Gm.		

Pecan Pear Pie: If desired, sprinkle pear pie filling with ½ cup of chopped pecans before dotting with margarine.

Per 1/7 Recipe

Calories	500	Sodium	164 mg.
Carbohydrate	57 Gm.	Potassium	520 mg.
Protein	6 Gm.	Cholesterol	0
Fat	17 Gm.		

RHUBARB MERINGUE PIE

1 baked 9-inch pastry shell
1 quart sliced rhubarb (2 lbs.)
½ cup water
2 cups sugar
⅓ cup cornstarch

1 teaspoon grated lemon peel
1 tablespoon lemon juice
1 teaspoon cinnamon
¼ teaspoon nutmeg

Cool pastry shell. Combine rhubarb and ¼ cup of the water in large saucepan. Cover and cook over medium heat for 10 minutes, or until rhubarb is tender and begins to come apart in strings. In small saucepan, mix sugar and cornstarch; stir in remaining ¼ cup of water. Stir over low heat until sugar dissolves and mixture begins to thicken; stir this into cooked rhubarb. Cook together over medium heat, stirring constantly until mixture is very thick and boiling. Boil, continuing to stir, for 1 minute. Remove from heat. Stir in lemon peel, juice, cinnamon and nutmeg. Turn into baked shell.

To Prepare Meringue:

3 egg whites, room temperature
¼ teaspoon Morton Lite Salt mixture

1 teaspoon lemon juice
¾ cup sugar

Beat egg whites and salt until foamy. Add lemon juice. Gradually beat in sugar, about 2 tablespoons at a time, and continue beating until very stiff and glossy. Invert a paper cup in center of pie. Spread meringue over filling, sealing well at pastry edge and spreading to rim of paper cup. Remove cup to leave open center. Bake at 350° for 12 to 15 minutes until lightly browned. Cool well. Makes one 9-inch pie.

Per 1/7 Recipe

Calories	468	Sodium	82 mg.
Carbohydrate	101 Gm.	Potassium	471 mg.
Protein	4 Gm.	Cholesterol	0
Fat	7 Gm.		

LEMON CHIFFON PIE

1 baked 9-inch pastry shell
1 envelope unflavored gelatin
⅔ cup lemon or lime juice
⅓ cup water
2 tablespoons sugar
1 teaspoon grated lemon peel

Yellow food coloring (optional)
3 egg whites
¼ teaspoon Morton Lite Salt mixture
½ cup light corn syrup

In a small saucepan, sprinkle gelatin over lemon juice and water. Add sugar. Heat over very low heat, stirring just until gelatin and sugar are completely dissolved. Remove from heat; stir in lemon peel and food coloring. Chill until mixture is the consistency of unbeaten egg white. Beat egg whites and salt until soft peaks form when beater is raised. Gradually add corn syrup, beating until stiff peaks form. Fold chilled gelatin mixture into beaten egg whites. If mixture is thick enough to mound at this point, pile lightly into pastry shell. If too thin, chill, stirring occasionally, until thick enough to mound. Pile into pastry shell. (Mixture may also be served in sherbet glasses.) Chill. Makes 1 pie.

Per 1/7 Recipe

Calories	284	Sodium	82 mg.
Carbohydrate	35 Gm.	Potassium	200 mg.
Protein	5 Gm.	Cholesterol	0
Fat	14 Gm.		

Each of the cakes which follow can be recommended to those who are concerned about what they eat. Perhaps the best choice for any special diet is the angel food cake, since it contains no egg yolks and no leavening.

ANGEL FOOD CAKE

1 cup sifted cake flour
About 1½ cups sugar
1½ cups egg white (12)
1½ teaspoons cream of tartar

¼ teaspoon Morton Lite Salt mixture
1½ teaspoons vanilla
½ teaspoon almond flavoring

Into a sifter, measure sifted cake flour and ¾ cup of the sugar. Sift these together 3 times. Into large bowl of electric mixer, measure egg whites; add cream of tartar and salt. Beat until foamy. While you beat, add remaining ¾ cup of sugar, 2 tablespoons at a time, and continue beating until the meringue holds stiff peaks. Fold in vanilla and almond. Gradually sift the flour-sugar mixture over the meringue, folding it in with a rubber spatula. Fold just until the flour-sugar mixture disappears. Push batter into ungreased tube pan, 10" × 4." Gently cut through batter with a knife. Bake at 375° until top springs back when lightly touched (about 35 to 40 minutes). Invert on a funnel. Let hang until cool. Makes one 10-inch tube cake.

Cherry Angel Food: Chop ½ cup of maraschino cherries and drain well on paper towel. Fold cherries into batter just before turning into tube pan.

Strawberry Glaze: Combine 2 cups of sifted confectioners' sugar, ⅛ teaspoon of Morton Lite Salt mixture, 2 teaspoons of lemon juice and ¼ cup of crushed fresh strawberries. Spread thinly over cake, letting it drip irregularly down sides.

Per 1/10 Cake

	Angel	Cherry Angel	With Strawberry Glaze
Calories	175	186	312
Carbohydrate	39 Gm.	41 Gm.	74 Gm.
Protein	5 Gm.	5 Gm.	5 Gm.
Fat	0	0	0
Sodium	84 mg.	84 mg.	98 mg.
Potassium	160 mg.	178 mg.	190 mg.
Cholesterol	0	0	0

YELLOW CAKE

2 cups sifted flour
2½ teaspoons baking powder
½ teaspoon Morton Lite Salt mixture
½ cup softened unsalted poly-unsaturated margarine

1 cup sugar
1 teaspoon vanilla
2 eggs
¾ cup milk

Sift flour, baking powder and salt together. Cream margarine with sugar and vanilla until light and fluffy. Add eggs, one at a time, beating well after each addition. Mix in sifted dry ingredients in 3 additions alternately with milk. Pour into 2 greased and floured 8-inch layer cake pans. Bake at 375° until cake springs back when lightly touched (20 to 25 minutes). Cool. Frost as desired. Makes two 8-inch layers.

Yellow Cake Square: Bake in 8" × 8" × 2" square pan for 40 minutes.

Spice Cake: Follow recipe above but add to dry ingredients before sifting ½ teaspoon of cinnamon, ¼ teaspoon of nutmeg and ¼ teaspoon of allspice.

Per 1/10 Cake

Calories	273	Sodium	74 mg.
Carbohydrate	38 Gm.	Potassium	120 mg.
Protein	4 Gm.	Cholesterol	56 mg.
Fat	12 Gm.		

SILVER CAKE

3 cups sifted cake flour
1½ cups sugar
4 teaspoons baking powder
1 teaspoon Morton Lite Salt mixture

¾ cup unsalted polyunsaturated margarine
¾ cup milk
4 egg whites
1½ teaspoons vanilla

Grease and lightly flour 2 round layer cake pans 9" × 1½". Sift together flour, sugar, baking powder and salt. In large bowl of electric mixer, beat margarine enough to soften. Add flour mixture and ½ cup of the milk. Beat 2 minutes on medium speed of electric mixer. Add egg whites, vanilla and remaining ¼ cup of milk. Beat 1 minute with electric mixer. Pour into prepared pans. Bake at 375° for 25 to 30 minutes, or until cake springs back when lightly touched. Cool on wire rack. Makes two 9-inch layers.

Note: Batter may also be baked in rectangular baking pan 13" × 9" × 2", or used to make 36 cupcakes.

Per 1/10 Cake

Calories	373	Sodium	341 mg.
Carbohydrate	55 Gm.	Potassium	221 mg.
Protein	43 Gm.	Cholesterol	2 mg.
Fat	16 Gm.		

APRICOT SKILLET CAKE

1 can (1 lb. 13 oz.) apricot halves
¼ cup dark corn syrup
½ cup softened unsalted poly-unsaturated margarine
⅓ cup brown sugar
1⅓ cups sifted flour

½ cup sugar
2 teaspoons baking powder
½ teaspoon Morton Lite Salt mixture
2 eggs
1 teaspoon vanilla
1 tablespoon lemon juice

Drain apricot halves; reserve ½ cup of syrup. Blend corn syrup, ¼ cup of the margarine, and brown sugar in 10-inch skillet. Arrange apricot halves in mixture, cut side down. Bake at 375° for 15 minutes. Meanwhile sift flour, sugar, baking powder and salt together into mixing bowl. Beat eggs in another bowl. Melt remaining ¼ cup of margarine. Blend eggs, apricot syrup, vanilla and melted margarine. Stir into dry ingredients; beat until smooth. Sprinkle lemon juice over apricots in skillet. Pour batter evenly over top. Bake at 375° for 25 to 30 minutes, or until cake has shrunk from sides of pan and toothpick inserted in center comes out clean. Cool for 5 minutes. Loosen sides of cake with spatula. Place a round platter over pan and invert together. Makes 8 servings.

Per Serving

Calories	391	Sodium	90 mg.
Carbohydrate	64 Gm.	Potassium	225 mg.
Protein	4 Gm.	Cholesterol	68 mg.
Fat	14 Gm.		

APPLESAUCE CAKE

1 cup softened unsalted poly-unsaturated margarine
1¾ cups sugar
3 cups unsifted flour
½ teaspoon Morton Lite Salt mixture
2 teaspoons baking soda

1 teaspoon baking powder
2 teaspoons cinnamon
1 teaspoon cloves
1 jar (15 oz.) applesauce
1 cup raisins
1 cup chopped walnuts
4 egg whites

In bowl, cream together margarine and sugar. Sift together flour, salt, baking soda, baking powder, cinnamon and cloves. Add to margarine mixture alternately with applesauce. Beat in raisins and walnuts. Beat egg white until soft peaks form. Fold into cake batter. Turn batter into well-greased 10-inch tube pan. Bake at 350° for 1 hour and 20 to 30 minutes, or until cake tester inserted in center of cake comes out clean. Cool for 10 minutes. Loosen cake carefully with spatula on all edges. Remove from pan and cool completely. If desired, dust top with confectioners' sugar. Makes one 10-inch tube cake or 18 servings.

Per Serving

Calories	328	Sodium	45 mg.
Carbohydrate	46 Gm.	Potassium	188 mg.
Protein	3 Gm.	Cholesterol	0
Fat	13 Gm.		

WHITE MOUNTAIN FROSTING

½ cup sugar
¼ cup light corn syrup
2 tablespoons water

2 stiffly beaten egg whites
1 teaspoon vanilla

In a very small saucepan, mix sugar, corn syrup and water. Cover; heat to rolling boil over medium heat. Remove cover and boil rapidly to 242° on a candy thermometer, or until syrup spins a 6- to 8-inch thread. This heats very quickly; egg whites should be ready before cooking. When mixture begins to boil, pour hot syrup very slowly in a thin stream into the beaten egg whites, beating constantly with an electric mixer at medium speed or with a rotary beater. Beat at high speed until stiff peaks form. Stir in vanilla during last minute of beating. Enough for two 8- or 9-inch layers, or a rectangular cake 13″ × 9″ × 2″.

Satiny Beige Frosting: Instead of ½ cup of granulated sugar, use ½ cup of brown sugar and decrease the vanilla to ½ teaspoon.

Mocha Frosting: Follow the recipe for Satiny Beige Frosting and, toward end of beating, stir in 1 teaspoon of instant coffee.

Per Recipe

Calories	652	Sodium	94 mg.
Carbohydrate	161 Gm.	Potassium	550 mg.
Protein	7 Gm.	Cholesterol	0
Fat	0		

Note: Variations have about the same nutrients as basic recipe.

CREAMY VANILLA FROSTING

⅓ cup unsalted polyunsaturated margarine, softened
3 cups sifted confectioners' sugar

About 2 tablespoons milk
1½ teaspoons vanilla

Beat margarine until creamy; gradually beat in sugar. Add only enough milk to bring to good spreading consistency. Stir in vanilla. Enough for two 8- or 9-inch layers or rectangular cake 13″ × 9″ × 2″.

Creamy Pineapple Frosting: Omit milk and vanilla. Instead stir in ⅓ cup of *well-drained,* canned crushed pineapple, blending well.

Creamy Orange (or Lemon) Frosting: Omit milk and vanilla. Add 1½ tablespoons of grated orange (or lemon) peel and about 3 tablespoons of orange (or lemon) juice.

Per Recipe

	Vanilla	Pineapple	Orange
Calories	2306	2346	2339
Carbohydrate	526 Gm.	539 Gm.	538 Gm.
Protein	1 Gm.	trace	trace
Fat	30 Gm.	29 Gm.	29 Gm.
Sodium	18 mg.	5 mg.	4 mg.
Potassium	40 mg.	130 mg.	140 mg.
Cholesterol	3 mg.	0	0

INDEX

218

Fine Products From
Morton Salt Company

Morton® Iodized and Plain Salt
Morton Lite Salt® mixture
Morton® Nature's Seasons® seasoning blend
Morton® Salt Substitute
Morton® Seasoned Salt Substitute
Morton® Salt and Pepper Shakers
Morton® Canning and Pickling Salt